How to Save
BIG MONEY
When You
LEASE
A CAR

How to Save BIG MONEY When You LEASE A CAR

MICHAEL FLINN

A PERIGEE BOOK

This book is for my mother.

Perigee Books
are published by
The Putnam Publishing Group
200 Madison Avenue
New York, NY 10016

Library of Congress Cataloging-in-Publication Data

Flinn, Michael, date.
How to save big money when you lease a car / Michael Flinn.
p.   cm.
ISBN 0-399-51609-3
Includes index
1. Automobiles, Rental—United States—Popular works.   I. Title.
HE5620.R45F57   1990   90-6757 CIP
388.32′0973—dc20

Printed in the United States of America

1 2 3 4 5 6 7 8 9 10

Contents

Introduction

Leasing is a way to drive and enjoy a brand-new car and still make an amazingly low monthly payment.

It is also a way for the friendly folks at your local car store to take you for a long and mysterious ride—at the end of which you say goodbye to a whole lot of money. Many people who lease cars spend hundreds, even thousands, of dollars more than necessary to drive the car they want.

The reason is simple: ignorance. Auto leasing is a black hole in consumer knowledge. More people know less about leasing a car than about almost any other common, everyday consumer transaction. And, in the car business, consumer ignorance generates money. When you are short on knowledge, you get taken for the long dollar.

Why don't people catch on? Low payments. Lease payments are normally so much lower than buy payments that customers, having entered a state of bliss, never realize that a ton of markup can be hidden in that low payment.

So customers—that is to say, you—believe salespeople when

they say they discounted a big chunk of money off the price of the car. You think you got a deal.

And you go away happy, after spending hundreds of dollars you don't even know about—and will never know about. For the price of your car will not appear on your lease contract.

As one of my managers used to say, "The great thing about leasing is, the customers can never figure it out."

He was right. And he was not talking about people who don't know their ears from their elbows. For example, I know a guy in his midtwenties who worked for a bank as a mortgage processor. He's sharp and he's thoroughly familiar with percentage rates, declining balances, the computation of monthly loan payments, and so on. One day, he went out to buy a $17,000 Ford Taurus. When the salesman told him it would cost him $430 a month, he went into shock.

Then, as he was coming out of shock, they told him he could lease the car for $323 a month plus tax. He grabbed the deal.

His lease payment was based on a price of approximately $16,500. Yet the original markup on the car was about $2,200. Twenty minutes of negotiation could have won him a price of $15,500 and saved him a thousand dollars.

But there was no way for him to figure out the price he was paying. Until now.

THE PURPOSE OF THIS BOOK

This book will help you save money when you lease. Now you'll be able to get that low payment and get a damn good deal as well. You will understand what you are doing—and what is being done to you.

To begin with, the book will provide definitions of some important terms and will answer many of the questions most frequently asked about leasing. It will acquaint you with the numbers and formulas commonly used in lease deals, tell you where to find them and how to use them, and show you how to figure some of them out from scratch. Frequently, in fact, the book will not simply tell you what to do, but also try to explain how to decide what to do.

In addition, it will provide guidelines to help you determine the value of your used car and to help you negotiate a good deal on the new car. For leasing a car is much like buying a car: Almost everything is negotiable. And therefore, anything you do not ask for or negotiate for will not be offered to you.

The book will also describe some of the tricks and scams you are likely to encounter. Now, we're not talking "crooked" here; the car business is, after all, the heartbeat of the American economy. And the dealership where I worked, called herein the East Babbit Ford Store, was a pillar-of-the-community sort of business. It was located in the western New York area, outside a city of about 320,000 people in a Metropolitan Area of approximately 1.5 million. And you might say it was centrally located: within a fifteen-minute-drive radius of the place, there were *eight* other Ford stores. The closest was only five minutes away. One of the others was the highest-volume Ford dealer in New York State. Competition was so intense that the area was a car shopper's paradise. And yet month in, month out, we were second or third in Ford sales in that vicinity.

The things I'll be telling you about, then, will be things I learned at a high-powered, high-volume dealership that sold the product of one of the wealthiest and most successful corporations in the world.

Unfortunately, there are many things you need to know that I cannot tell you. You need to know, for example, the dealer cost on the car you want; the residual values placed on that car by various lenders at that particular time; the lease rates being used by various lenders at that time; and the value of your old car when you sell it or trade it in. Although I can't tell you these things in advance, I will tell you how to find them out.

Do take the trouble to find out. To make your best deal, you have to do your homework.

ONE

What's It All About?

Let's begin with a couple of bird's-eye views of the whole process and some useful definitions.

In some ways, leasing and buying are quite similar.

- You make a deal; that is, you agree on an amount of money to be paid for a car and sign a contract.
- A lender, usually a bank, a savings-and-loan, an auto manufacturer's credit company, or some other financing agency advances that money and you drive away in the car.
- You pay back that sum of money plus interest in regular monthly payments.

The main differences are:

- The number of legal controls government has placed on the transaction. Leasing has fewer.
- The time it takes for you to pay back the amount you owe. With leasing, you pay back much more slowly.

- The degree of risk taken by the lender. Leasing is considered riskier. First, there can be more money at stake, for leasing can generate higher profits than installment loans. Second, whatever the profit, the original amount invested takes longer to recover.

When you mix these differences and shake gently, the result is leasing's major drawback in comparison to buying.

If you pay off a buy loan early, most installment purchase contracts require you to pay only the remaining principal—what's left of the original amount lent to you. The uncollected interest is forgone.

But if you end a lease before the term is up, many lessors will apply charges over and above the amount they originally put out, which usually equals the purchase price of the car. In cases of early termination, lease contracts often specify that you pay some or all of the remaining interest charges, plus a penalty, plus some or all of the car's future estimated value.

Later, we'll discuss excessive charges for early termination in more detail and talk about how to minimize them.

Despite the differences between leasing and buying, a leased car is a sold car. Says who? Say the manufacturer, the dealer, and the salesperson.

When a salesperson leases a car, it goes away; it is gone. These expressions mean sold and delivered. Sold and delivered means the salesperson's commission is due.

The same goes for the dealer: The car is sold. The dealer submits the lease contract to the lessor and is paid cash; he pays off whoever financed the car, whether factory or bank, and the rest is profit; or, if you trade a car in, he has your trade-in to sell for profit; and he is rid of all responsibility for the new car.

Except, that is, in some cases, when the dealer, acting as an agent of the lessor, receives the car when you turn it in. Then he fills out a report describing the car's condition and collects any money you owe the lessor for damage or excess mileage.

In return for acting as the lessor's agent, the dealer gains the opportunity to sell the car, to you or to someone else, as a used car for as much profit as he can get. However, the dealer is not required to sell the car, or to repair the car, or to wash and wax the car, or anything else.

When the lease expires, the lessor, which is almost always the financing agency involved, owns the car. If the dealer cannot or does not want to sell it, the financing agency must take the responsibility and risk of realizing the money represented by its residual value, or the estimated value of the car when the lease expires.

At the East Babbit Ford Store, the financing agency for the vast majority of our leases was Ford Motor Credit Company, a lending institution owned by Ford.

If you leased a car from us, here's how the transaction would shape up. The factory, Ford, would sell the car to the East Babbit Ford Store. Somebody, in our case usually Ford Credit, would pay Ford, financing our purchase. When you leased it from us, we would sell it to Ford Credit. Ford Credit would then pay off themselves (or whoever did finance it for us) and pay us the profit, if any. Then, Ford Credit, acting as both lender and lessor, would, in effect, sell you a portion of the car's life—a block of time, which equals a block of money. And then, of course, Ford Credit would collect the monthly payments that paid off that block of money.

From your point of view as a customer, when you lease a car you buy the use of it for a certain amount of time. That time equals a certain percentage of the car's "life expectancy." And that time is convertible to a certain percentage of the car's monetary value, or retail price. You pay X dollars to buy a certain percentage of the car's life.

This is the reason lease payments are so low. You pay for only that portion of the car's life which you use. Since this is considerably less than the full value of the car, you also pay less in sales taxes.

UNITS OF MONEY: DEFINITIONS OF THE COMPONENT PARTS OF A LEASE DEAL

In order to convert a fraction of a car's life to an amount of money, you have to begin with an amount that represents its full-life value.

Full-life value equals a retail price.

When the dealer figures your lease payment he bases it on a retail price. That price can be the full sticker price of the car ("full pop"), it can be more than the sticker price, or it can be a discounted price, as low as a hundred or two over dealer cost. There is no one set lease price or lease payment. On a car that retails for (has a sticker price of) $10,000, the fraction of value you use up can be a fraction of $10,000, or a fraction of a discounted price of $9,100. Your lease payment may be based on a price that is a good deal for you or a good deal for the dealer. It is a matter of negotiation.

So the purchase price on which your lease payment is based is the first important amount, or unit, of money in a lease deal. This is also known as the *sell price*, the *deal price*, or, when there's no trade-in or down payment, the *acquisition cost*, the *capitalized cost* (*cap cost*), the *net agreed value*, and a number of other things.

The next important unit is the *Manufacturer's Suggested Retail Price* (MSRP) *before* deductions for option package discounts. Options package or options group discounts are factory discounts off the total price of a preselected group of options. You don't pick 'em: The options in the group are determined by the manufacturer. Some packages contain only a few options, the total price of which is discounted only $50 to $100. Others contain ten or more, with a discounted price many hundreds of dollars lower than the total of all the options in the group.

In this book we will use MSRP *not* to mean sticker or list price, but to mean the manufacturer's suggested price before the package discount is subtracted. Sticker price or list price (also sometimes called the MSRP on the window sticker) will mean the car's price *after* the discount is deducted. It is important to separate these two prices because the MSRP before the discount is the amount most lenders use to calculate the car's residual value.

Next, then, is the car's residual value. Ford calls it *lease-end value*. Others call it the *end-of-term value*. Whatever it's called, this is what the lessor, or lender, thinks the car will be worth when the lease expires. It is calculated as a percentage of MSRP before the manufacturer's discounts. It differs from car to car, and for most cars with most lenders it goes down every two months following the month of the car's introduction. It, too, is used to calculate your payment, and the larger it is the lower your payment.

Next is the amount your payment pays off before interest or lease charges, leasing's equivalent to the principal on a loan. Most lenders call this the car's "depreciation"; a few term it the "capitalized cost." Most lenders who call it "depreciation" use the term "capitalized cost" to refer to the car's purchase price.

Then there is the *lease-end buyout*, or *payoff*. This is the amount, written into the contract, that you agree to pay if you wish to buy the car at the end of the lease. It may be equal to the residual value, or it may be that fraction of the car's purchase price which you have not paid off. Or it may be some other figure. What figure? A figure you never discover.

If the lease-end buyout equals the residual value, that amount is usually equivalent to a high estimated future *retail* price, a price the lessor *hopes* the car will bring on the market. If you agree to that buyout, you agree to the lessor's dream price.

In addition, there can be, and often is, another, lower, unmentioned buyout, normally equal to estimated future wholesale value of the car. This is the amount of money the lessor must get in order to make an acceptable return on investment.

Finally, there is the buyout or payoff during the term of the lease. Since you are essentially paying off the capitalized cost of the car, there should not be a prepayment penalty. Normally, however, there is. It's called an early-termination penalty, and most banks charge one. Chrysler Credit charges one. General Motors Acceptance Corporation (GMAC) used to, but now does not. Ford charges one, but in my experience the dealer can usually persuade them to forgo it.

Obviously, prepayment penalty or not, your during-the-term buyout decreases as you make your payments. Not so obvious is the fact that you may never know what it really is. Depending on whom you lease from, some of the people who do know will refuse to tell you. And others who know will lie. This leads to an interesting question.

How Well Are You Protected by the Consumer Credit Act of 1976?

This is the legislation that requires lenders to disclose points and other fees on loans, along with the true interest rate. If you lease, the act grants you some protection but not much. The act unreasonably differentiates between installment purchases and leases. Why? Either the writers of the legislation did not fully understand time as a commodity (unlikely) or suave lobbyists whispered honeyed words. For a lease to be considered a "credit sale" and thus for the lessee to receive the full protection of the law, the lessee must pay a sum at least as great as the value of the property.

Now, it is possible to end up paying that much. But since the reason to lease a car is to possess the best years of the property's life, to have and use it while it's "nice," for a sum less than its full value, leasing can never be considered a credit sale as long as there's a good reason to do it.

In the practical world, leasing is nothing but a credit sale, another way to finance a car. Leasing a car is not like renting part of a building. The building will go on existing into the indefinite future. But a car has a very limited and predictable lifespan. You are buying a fraction of it, and a fairly accurate numerical value can be put on that fraction.

In the view of the legal world, however, the lessor is renting you property rather than selling you time or a known fraction of the life of a commodity. From the lessor's point of view, this is a good thing. He receives additional tax breaks. And at the same time his responsibility to you decreases. Renters, you see, have reduced status in the eyes of the law.

You, too, get a tax break. In most states, you pay sales or use tax each month on the amount of your payment. This usually amounts to less than you'd pay on a buy, and you pay it over a long period of time.

But that's the only break you get. When you lease, thanks to your legal status as renter, the Consumer Credit Act does *not* require the lessor to disclose the actual interest rate being charged. It does not require the lessor to divulge its true estimate of the vehicle's future value when the lease expires. Nor does it require the lessor to tell you the actual balance owed when the lease expires.

So you can be conned. It is as though, after paying your mortgage for ten years, the bank would not tell you what you still owed on your house and instead, you had to ask the person who sold it to you. Then you paid whatever that person said, and they paid off the bank. Do you think that person would add a few extra scoots, a little juice, for themselves? It's conceivable, isn't it. Now, what if that person were a car dealer?

The Consumer Credit Act does give you some protection. The lessor is legally required to state that the lease is a lease (i.e., that you must return the car); how much cash, if any, must be paid up front; the number of payments and the total amount of those payments; your liability, if any, for the difference between estimated and actual market value of the vehicle at the end of the lease; if you do have such liability, how the amount will be determined; and whether or not you have an option to purchase, and if so, at what time and at what price.

As you can see, the act protects you from the consumer

equivalent of armed robbery. But without requirements to disclose APR (Annualized Percentage Rate—for practical purposes, the interest rate actually being paid), or to disclose the actual estimated lease end value and exact balance owed, the act does not protect you from being fast-talked, faked out, bamboozled, flimflammed, jived, jerked around, lied to, and fundamentally conned.

TWO

Common Questions About Leasing

Who Leases?

Anybody who wants or needs to. Once upon a time, leasing was considered proper mainly for professionals: doctors, lawyers, businessmen, corporate fleet managers, and so on. But now leasing is simply another method of mass consumer auto financing. Anybody and everybody does it.

From my friend the mortgage processor, a guy in his mid-twenties . . .

. . . to a middle-aged parochial-school teacher who made little money, had never had a new car in her life, and was ready to wipe out her savings account so she could afford buy payments . . .

. . . to a youngish guy in the computer business who made a lot of money but wanted to put out as little of it as possible and still have a superfancy, down-sized sport truck . . .

. . . to a successful pig farmer who wanted to cruise the countryside in a full-sized, four-wheel-drive pickup truck that was loaded to the max.

In terms of numbers of people who lease autos, the estimates vary wildly. One "expert" source pegs the number at just under .75 million (individual consumers, excluding corporate fleet deals), while another estimates 2.5 million. On the basis of an estimate given by the National Automobile Dealers' Association, I'd guess that in the last few years a little over one million people a year have been leasing cars instead of buying them. The numbers are soft because manufacturers report leased cars as retail sales.

WHY LEASE?

People lease to get lower monthly payments. Car companies began to promote mass consumer leasing at a time when rising prices and interest rates were putting car payments beyond the reach of many people. With leasing, you pay less because you pay only for the portion of the life value of the car that you use up. Thus a new car becomes affordable. Or a new car plus other things. Or a bigger car, or a car with more options. Or, in some states, where the payment for a leased car does not show up as a debt on credit reports, you get a new car and still have those thousands of dollars of credit available.

These benefits are real and substantial. If you want or need them, they are worth money. *And if you know how to negotiate a good deal on a lease,* you will get these benefits for less than they are worth, even if leasing costs you a few hundred more than the best you could do on a buy.

IS THERE A BEST LENGTH-OF-LEASE TERM?

Leases commonly run three, four, five years. No particular term is best. A two-year lease might be just what you need, or a five-year lease might be best.

The length I'll talk most about is four years, or 48 months.

The principles are the same, no matter what the term, and where I worked, and with the mass-market cars I sold, 48-month leases were the most common.

This makes sense, I think. With average mileage accumulation of 12,000 to 15,000 a year, a car should remain in reasonably good shape through its fourth year. After 55,000 to 60,000 miles, however, pieces of the car all too often start to break.

If the manufacturer's powertrain warranty covers the car for 60,000 miles and you drive 50,000 to 60,000 in four years, you will have warranty protection for a majority of the most expensive repairs during the entire term of a four-year lease with no added cost for an extended warranty.

But if leasing for five years is the only way to afford the car you want and its warranty will expire during the fifth year, you have a choice. Either you pay the price of an extended warranty or run the risk of suffering a major expense for repairs.

Here are a few more remarks about the common lease terms.

Two- and Three-Year Leases

In the case of heavy business use, with mileage piling up at the rate of 20,000 or 30,000 miles per year, two- and three-year leases are the terms of choice. After 60,000 or so miles, many cars start to go downhill rather rapidly. A car leased for four years and driven 25,000 miles a year may not be the car you want it to be during its fourth year.

High mileage, however, will raise your lease payment. Most leases are figured at 15,000 miles per year of lease term. If you exceed that, Ford charges 6¢ a mile for each and every excessive mile. Chrysler, GMAC, and most banks charge 8¢ a mile. Some banks charge as much as 15¢ a mile. With the typical 6¢ to 8¢ penalty, driving 25,000 miles a year will cost you an additional $600 to $800 a year, or $50 to $66 a month. This is not a trifling amount. Nevertheless, here's an example of what a short term-lease can do, even with a penalty for high mileage.

Suppose you receive a $300-a-month car allowance from

your employer. Your job involves a lot of customer contact and you want to drive the nicest car possible. You don't mind paying a little out of your own pocket—but not much.

You've been looking at a Taurus or a Cutlass or similar car that lists for $13,300 after a $500 options package discount off the original MSRP. You've worked a deal at a local dealership for a price of $11,979. You drive 25,000 miles a year: You won't want the car any longer than three years.

After adding the 6% sales tax, a three-year buy at 10.5% will cost you $412.68 per month. According to the Ford Motor Credit lease charts for a Taurus, your three-year lease payment will be $315—including tax and a $50 per month penalty for excess mileage.

So there you are, driving a nice car to impress your customers, which is indeed helpful, and putting out $15 a month of your own money instead of $112.

To match that payment on a buy, you'd have to purchase a car for about $9,150 that listed for, tops, $10,300. You'd be driving three thousand dollars' less car. Obviously, it would lack many of the features that are so enjoyable, and so impressive, on the thirteen-three glam-o-ride.

Incidentally, if you are interested in short-term leases, check to see if the manufacturer's credit arm is offering bargain rates. Manufacturers occasionally offer super deals on two-year leases in order to accelerate the trading cycle and sell more cars. By "super," I mean lease rates of 2.5% to 3%, compared to rates of 9.5% to 11%. You may have to ask about this. Some dealers, believing few customers want very short leases, will not spend the money to advertise short-term bargain rates. But if the rates are in effect, you can save $50 or more per month.

To give you an idea of cost to you per lease term, I'll include examples of payments for a $12,000 car and a $30,000 car. These payments are calculated with a 10% lease rate, and the residual value (or lease-end value) factors come from September–October charts—i.e., the very beginning of the model year, when residual values are highest and lease payments lowest.

Two-year payment, $12,000 car, 47% residual: $338.56/mo.
$30,000 car, 51% residual: $801.27/mo.
$12,000 car at 2.75% rate: $285.29/mo.
Three-year payment, $12,000 car, 40% residual: $270.06/mo.
$30,000 car, 45% residual: $639.59/mo.

Four-Year Leases

Four years represents the basic compromise among lowness of payment, length of warranty coverage, and reliability of vehicle.

Four-year payment, $12,000 car, 33% residual: $234.05/mo.
$30,000 car, 39% residual: $555.01/mo.

Five-Year Leases

Advantage: low payment. Disadvantage: possible unreliability and high maintenance costs during the fifth year. Another possible disadvantage is that you may be sick of the car after four years.

Advertisements often feature five-year payments, for the low payment gives the ad more impact and brings the car within the reach of more people. Dealers are required by law, however, to specify the length of term used to calculate the payment. You will find the length of term in the barely visible print at the bottom of the ad.

Five-year payment, $12,000 car, 28% residual: $208.05/mo.
$30,000 car, 34% residual: $497.51/mo.

Five-and-a-Half-Year or 66-Month Leases

These have been available nationwide for some time for expensive vehicles, but for low- and medium-priced vehicles they are relatively new, and quite new in the East. They have the same advantages and disadvantages as five-year leases, only more so.

. If you are tempted by a 66-month lease, check it carefully. Some such leases advertise astoundingly low payments, but give you astoundingly low mileage allowances. One, for example, allows 41,250 total miles. Over 66 months, that's 7,500 miles a year: *half* that included with the payments for the two- to five-year leases cited above. Exceeding the allowance brings a charge of 8¢ to 15¢ per mile. This could lead to an unpleasant surprise.

If you need a lease ending in the half-year, e.g. eighteen, thirty, or forty-two months, many lessors offer them.

Can the Length of the Lease Term Cause a Problem?

Yes. Cars provoke strong emotions. They tend to be loved or hated. And, as we all know, love can turn into hate with surprising speed. And other circumstances can change just as rapidly.

The problem arises if feelings or circumstances change halfway through the lease. Because the monthly payment is so low, it pays off much less of the principal owed on the car: what must be paid to clear your debt.

With either a four-year lease or a four-year buy, if you want out after a year and a half the chances are very good that you'll have to come up with cash out of your pocket to pay off the note. But since you pay $50 to $100 a month less on the lease, the chunk of cash needed will be hefty indeed. You may not have it. You may be stuck for quite some time with a car you hate.

Before leasing, try to assess your need for the car and the length of time your affection for it will actually last.

Is Leasing Good for Me If My Credit Is Bad?

No. In general, you need better credit to lease than you do to buy on time. Why? Because not only is the lender trusting you to repay the money, it is also trusting you to return the car in reasonably good shape. Since they're trusting you more, it takes less to scare them away.

Many lenders, however, will permit cosigners on a lease, and your income does not have to be as high as you may have heard. Some lenders stipulate a minimum income of $25,000 a year. Others will be satisfied if you earn $16,000, and sometimes manufacturers' credit companies will be satisfied with less, if there is a creditworthy cosigner.

WHO PAYS FOR INSURANCE AND NONWARRANTY REPAIRS?

You do. If you lease, you are responsible for repairing and insuring the car.

DOES THE MANUFACTURER'S WARRANTY COVER A LEASED CAR?

Yes. You receive all the protection the warranty affords.

This is also true with any extended warranties you may purchase. Drivers who will put on less than 60,000 miles during the lease term probably don't need an extended warranty. Drivers who will drive more than 60,000 miles during the lease may save money with an extended warranty.

A tip: If your car is loaded with motor-driven options (power this and power that), see if the manufacturer's warranty will cover them for the term of your lease. If it doesn't, try to find out how often they break on that model. If many of these options have a reputation for breaking often and early, check the price of an extended warranty that covers them. You will have some time to do this; most extended warranty plans can be purchased up to 12 months after you take the car.

Does Leasing Require Me to Carry More Insurance?

Generally speaking, no . . . But: Most leases have an insurance requirement of $50,000 property damage, $100,000 to 300,000 bodily injury liability insurance, and comprehensive and collision insurance with a maximum deductible of $500.

In areas of the country where auto insurance is not tremendously expensive, this is pretty much a standard policy, the policy that most people have.

In areas like Philadelphia, however, where auto insurance is tremendously expensive, buying on an installment loan may enable you to save money on insurance. Installment purchase contracts require you to carry insurance; in fact, the lender wants you to have the same coverage as on a lease. But buy contracts rarely specify the amounts of required coverage. And the lenders rarely check to see if you have any at all. On a buy, you may be able to get away with reducing your coverage and save a significant amount of money.

Check insurance costs in your area for different amounts of coverage. Check with local lenders to find out how much coverage is required on their installment-purchase contracts. Then check with the department of motor vehicles to see what your state requires. The state may have a requirement that overrides any differences between lease and purchase contracts.

Do Low Factory Finance Rates and Cash Rebates Apply When You Lease?

Interest rate buydowns (low financing) normally apply only to installment-purchase loans. But once in a while a manufacturer will lower the rate on its credit company's leases. Don't expect this, but check for it. Ask about it at the dealership, for the dealer will not tell you automatically. He'll go with the lender who pays him the most, whether or not it costs you more.

On the other hand, cash rebates almost always come with the car, not the method of financing. So when you lease, you get the rebate. And since the cash comes from the manufacturer, the rebate applies whether you lease from a dealership or a lease store.

Factory cash back is your money; the factory pays it to you. This means that you decide how to use it. You can sign the check over to the dealer and use it as cash down to lower your lease payment. Or you can walk out of the store with the check in your pocket. You can even use it to lower the lease buyout, if you know that you'll be buying the car later—although in most cases this would be a bad idea. Money now is worth more than money three to five years from now.

If you can handle the payment without putting money down, think of the rebate as money in the bank, able to earn interest for you. Compare what you will earn with what you'll save if you put it down on the car.

WHAT'S THE DIFFERENCE BETWEEN OPEN- AND CLOSED-END LEASES?

Open-End Leases

With an open-end lease, the vehicle has no preset value when the lease expires. Its value is determined by the market—even if you simply return the car to the lessor. When the lease expires, the residual value estimated four years ago is compared to what that model is going for now.

Going for where? At what price? At fair market price? What does that mean? Wholesale? Retail? If retail, at what degree of discount? Who decides?

As you can see, there's many a catch in an open-end lease. And, once, many people got caught. When a lease had expired someone would bring back a car. A guy at the dealership or lease store would look at it. Then he'd look at some charts. Then he'd hold out his hand and ask for money. Lots of it.

Now, open-end leases are comparatively rare. But some banks still offer them and a few lease stores still push them. So watch out. Unless your circumstances are unusual, it's best to avoid any lease without a preset residual value.

Closed-End Leases (with an Option to Buy)

With a closed-end lease, you owe nothing at the end of the lease if you return the car. Except, perhaps, for that cracked windshield you thought the dealer might pay for. He won't. If the lease contains an end-of-term purchase option, permitting you to buy the car when the lease expires, most of today's lease contracts will specify the purchase price. Specified though it is, it may not be the "real" price required by the lender, so it may be negotiable. More about this later.

The leases you encounter will probably be closed-end, but check to be sure.

WHAT FEATURES SHOULD I LOOK FOR IN A CLOSED-END LEASE?

Disposition Fees

First, a feature to watch out for. Disposition fees, presumably to cover the cost of disposing of the car, create the exception to the rule just stated. Some bank leases charge them *whenever* you turn in the car, and they can be as high as $350 to $400.

If you come across a deal with a disposition fee, check the total of the monthly payments against the same total on deals without the fee offered by other lenders. Make sure the payment total plus the disposition fee is not significantly higher than the total payout on the other deals.

The Lease-End Purchase Option

Some lenders offer closed-end leases that automatically include a lease-end purchase option. Other lenders make it a feature you must choose and, in some cases, pay for. Yet others do not offer it at all.

The purchase option is a good thing if the price is right.

- The car may be the best you've ever had.
- The car may have "a big book" (hold its value unusually well and be worth a lot of money), enabling you to profit from buying and reselling it.

When comparing lease deals, check to see if the purchase option is there. If it's optional, compare the cost with and without it, and then compare the cost with it to other leases that include it automatically.

Typical Provisions for the End-of-Term Purchase Price

- Price preset at the official residual value (which you may be able to negotiate down) and written into the contract.
- Price not preset, but is determined later on the basis of "fair market value," which means the average of retail and whole-sale prices, reflecting "clean or average values."

The latter provision shows how the lease-end purchase price was determined on pre-1989 GMAC lease contracts. It contains a tantalizing ambiguity: The difference between "clean" and "average" can be more than $1,500. No one, least of all you, could have known what the price would be.

Now, however, the GMAC lease-end buyout price is preset. You may safely assume, I believe, that it will be preset at a fairly high retail number. It may be negotiable.

CURRENT GMAC LESSEES TAKE NOTE: GMAC's avowed purpose in changing their contract was to offer customers a better deal—thus to attract more customers. If you attempt to pay off a pre-1989 GMAC lease and the dealer tries to charge you "fair market price" for the car, mention this. Mention it often.

Does a preset lease-end purchase price necessarily mean a

good deal for you? No. You want it to, of course, and you also want it to be accurate, that is, to include no unstated profit for the middleman (dealer or lease store). For, even if you do not buy the car at the end of the lease, this buyout or purchase price will be your "nut"; it will determine whether or not you can make any money by selling the car.

Getting a lease-end purchase price that is both accurate and a decent deal may not be easy, but it sure is worth a try. Later, we'll talk about how to go about trying.

Voluntary Early Termination or Early Buyout

Finally, you want—but may not be able to have—the purchase option, with no prepayment penalty, to be in effect throughout the lease term.

Not many people buy out their leases ahead of time, so why is this important? Well, things change. For example, I know two families who have leased trucks. At the moment I write, both trucks have been sitting unused for months. These trucks will continue to sit; the people will continue to pay.

There are two ways out of this situation, two forms of voluntary early termination. One is to return the vehicle and pay the balance owed. The other, usually less expensive, is to sell the vehicle and use the proceeds to pay or help pay the balance owed. But you cannot sell the car unless the contract permits you to buy it.

Many bank leases flatly forbid early buyouts. Banks want to collect all the interest. A bank in Pennsylvania not only prohibits early buyouts, but also places you in default if you must terminate the lease early and requires you to return the car and pay all of the remaining lease payments, including interest.

The requirements of other lessors range from one extreme—no buyout, return the car, make all the payments, pay a penalty, and be responsible for the residual value—to the other, which is more favorable to you: buyout or lease payoff permitted for the balance of the purchase price with no penalties. And, oddly, some are so vague you can't tell what they require.

Typical Early Termination or Early Buyout Provisions Some of these provisions may change by the time you read this, but most will not. You will probably encounter, or may already have encountered, a contract containing some combination of them.

Ford Credit's lease contracts say nothing about early buyouts. They do permit voluntary early termination, but require that you return the car. You then owe an early termination fee of $200, plus something expressed in a way that makes it as incomprehensible as is humanly possible.

The gist of it: Your lease payment is divided into two parts, depreciation (the loss in value caused by age and wear) and interest, or "lease charges" (see "How to Calculate Lease Payments," page 97). If you terminate a Ford lease early, you owe the remaining depreciation, plus the residual value, minus the agreed-upon wholesale value of the car.

The kickers, not peculiar to Ford but present in most leases, are

- The early termination fee.
- Your obligation for the residual value, which may or may not add a big lump to the total. It depends on how the residual is calculated, or, since there are sometimes two, which one is used.
- The fact that you pay off depreciation more slowly than you think. You pay off any loan more slowly than you think, but more so on leases. You see, the way earned interest is calculated is not the same as on home mortgages and many other consumer loans. With the method used on leases, more interest is earned faster. When more money goes to pay interest, less goes to pay depreciation. Obviously, more depreciation remains for you to pay.

Ford Credit's practice *has been* to forgo extra charges, and terminate for the balance of the purchase price, if you press your dealer to ask for it.

With or without extra charges, however, it would be better for you to sell the car for even a very low retail figure and apply the proceeds to the lease payoff than to have the payoff reduced to an even lower wholesale figure.

To sell the car, however, you must be able to buy it, that is, pay off the lease without returning the car. Ford leases make no mention of your buying the car. They don't say you can, and they don't say you can't. They sort of fudge the point.

Chrysler Credit's leases likewise do not mention a purchase option during the term. In fact, they go further, stating that you have no right to early termination, period. But they then fudge this by adding, "Unless it is agreed in writing" by you, the dealer, and Chrysler Credit.

If everybody does agree that you can terminate early, the contract states that you will have to pay all of the remaining monthly payments with no rebate for unearned interest, plus the residual value (which Chrysler calls the "estimated end-of-term wholesale value") minus the amount Chrysler receives when it sells the car.

But this, too, can be changed, if, once again, it is agreed to in writing by you, the dealer, and Chrysler Credit.

It may seem that Chrysler is trying to create maximum confusion. In fact, however, the purpose of Chrysler's "fudging," like Ford's, is to allow the leasing dealer some room to negotiate.

And thus it allows you some room to negotiate. If the store wants your business, and it does, you may be able to negotiate a clause stating that you can buy out (pay off) the lease during the term for the balance of the purchase price without penalties.

As mentioned, GMAC has changed their contract. Previously, they permitted you to buy during the course of the lease. The price was high and there were penalties of $600 during the first year, $400 during the second, and $200 during the third.

Now, the penalties are gone—but so is your right to purchase during the lease term. This is a loss. However, like most other things in the mass-market auto world, it is probably negotiable.

Although you can't buy and thus can't sell the car, you do have the right to early termination without specific penalties. What you owe will be the sum of the remaining payments, minus the unearned lease charges (or unearned interest), and minus *the surplus of the sale price* after GMAC wholesales the car. The "surplus of the sale price" equals the amount over and above the residual value. This is a somewhat tricky way of saying that you are responsible for the amount of the residual value.

Heavy charges for early termination are among the bugaboos of leasing. You cannot know what will happen a few months from now, let alone a few years. So before doing a deal, get the lender's lease contract and read it. If it contains items that may hang you in the future, have them explained till you understand them thoroughly. Then try to negotiate them out of the contract.

Negotiating the Early Termination Tell the people at the car or lease store that you want them to help you get a better deal on this from the lender.

How do you decide what the deal should be? What would be a fair price for the buyout or payoff on an early termination? The same amount it would cost to pay off a regular installment loan for the amount of the lease acquisition cost (or capitalized cost, if your lender uses that term).

When you are doing the deal, you do not know if or when you may need to terminate early. So all you can do is have language similar to the above written into the contract.

When actually trying to terminate the lease ahead of time, you have to figure out a number: you have to know what it would cost to pay off a loan in the amount of the acquisition cost after x number of months. Here's a way to do it.

For your interest rate, use the current rate around town, or the going rate at the time you leased the car, whichever is lower. (If

the lessor accepts this approach, they will want to use whichever
is higher. You'll have to dicker over this.) To calculate the
interest earned on the amount, use the "interest on the declining
balance method." This is nothing special; it is the way interest
has been calculated on most loans since the Consumer Credit
Act forced lenders to disclose the true *Annualized Percentage
Rate* (APR).

For the amount of the loan, use the amount of your lease
acquisition cost or capitalized cost (see pages 100–102). To get
the remaining balance you can use a financial calculator, if you
have one, or a loan amortization chart, which can be found in
the back of a loan payment book. If you have neither, call a
bank. Tell them the amount of the loan, the percentage rate, the
length of the loan—the same length as your lease—and ask
what the payment would be. After you get the payment, ask for
the balance remaining after the number of months that have
gone by in your lease. They'll give you the answers.

Now you have to add in what you would have paid on the
loan but did not pay on the lease because of its lower payments.

To figure out that amount, subtract the before-tax lease payment from the loan payment. Then multiply the difference by
the number of months your lease has run. The result will be the
amount you haven't paid, but would have on the loan. Add it to
the balance owed quoted by the bank. This will give you approximately what it would cost to pay off a loan made to you; in other
words, what the lessor would make on money lent to you. Thus,
it is a number to shoot for as fair.

Now, to be a bit more fair, you would have to add about 1% of
the original loan amount to account for interest earned on a
balance which has been reduced more slowly by the lower lease
payment.

Since, however, you will be told simply "that is not how we do
it," your goal is to start a negotiation, not to be completely fair.
When they tell you they don't figure the balance owed the way
you have, respond by saying that your salesperson told you that
buying out your lease would work out to a total cost about the

same as it would be had you bought the car in the first place. Many salespeople have been taught to sell leasing by saying precisely that, so your salesperson may well have said it. And that's what you have figured out: what it would cost to pay off the deal had you bought the car in the first place. This amount should be considerably less than the contract calls for. To figure out how much less, you would have to learn how to calculate interest earned according to the rule of 78's, or according to the daily outstanding balance—beyond our limits of time and space here.

Bear in mind the following:

1. The car store or lease store wants both good word of mouth and repeat business. They'll probably try to help you. However, they may also try to help themselves by inflating the balance owed so they can make a profit. More about this later.

2. Your lessor will almost always be a lender who also makes regular installment purchase loans. The amount you negotiate for may provide less profit than hoped for on a lease. But that profit will nevertheless be one the lender is accustomed to. So don't believe your salesperson if she tells you that it simply can't be done because the lessor will not make enough money. Or don't believe him or her the first time, anyway. Not all lenders will negotiate these points. But some will, so try.

3. Do be willing to pay a bit more than the price you decided was fair. If you can negotiate a compromise for less than the stipulations of the contract require, you have won.

But Won't I Be Better Off Owning the Car?

It depends on the meaning of "own" and "better off." This question is usually voiced as an objection or a complaint.

The complaint has two parts.

The Idea of Ownership, Part One

First, the person feels that they will be deprived of the pride of ownership. But neither a lessee nor an installment purchaser will own the car anyway. The feeling of ownership is basically science fiction: a form of time travel. One projects oneself into a happy future when all the payments have been made.

If you are buying on time, you must pay off the loan and obtain a lien release before you own the car. As long as your car is under lien, the lien holder owns it.

And not only does the lien holder have the right to take the car away from you if you fail to make your payments; he can also tell you what to do with the car while you're making them.

Here are a few examples, taken from the back side of a typical bank installment purchase contract:

- You must keep the car insured, policies payable to the bank.
- You may not transfer, abandon, or substantially modify the car without written consent from the bank.
- You may not remove the car from the state for more than one month without the bank's written consent.
- You may not move to another state without the bank's written consent.

Think that one over, folks.

"Own" the car? When you sign up to "buy" a car on time, you lose ownership of yourself. You lose some of your rights as an American citizen. Of course, this is unconstitutional. But how much would it cost to prove it?

The Idea of Ownership, Part Two: Equity

For all practical purposes, equity is simply the amount of money you can get for something over and above what you owe on it and what it costs you to sell it. What you get minus what you pay for debt and selling cost equals your equity—whether the object be a house, a car, or a pair of underpants.

The second part of the idea of ownership is that when you buy on time you can recover some of your money by cashing in the equity your payments have built up in the vehicle.

But the value of most cars declines rapidly. The equity built up through monthly buy payments may be less than you expect and must be compared to the "equity in cash" achieved by the monthly savings of a lease.

CAN YOU HAVE EQUITY IN A LEASED VEHICLE?

Yes. And if you have it, you can cash it in—as long as the lease has a purchase option. Often, however, you will have had to negotiate the buyout down to make that equity available to yourself. If you have to pay the lessor a high retail price, you'll have to get a *very* high retail price to make any money.

Selling a leased car is the same as selling any car that is under lien. A few months before the lease is up, find out the amount of the lease payoff and compare it to the amount you can get for the car. If you can get more than you have to pay (assuming you have a closed-end lease with an option to buy), you sell the car, pay off the lease, and pocket the profit.

If you can't, you turn the car in.

WILL LEASING COST MORE IN THE LONG RUN?

It may, or it may not. It depends on the kind of car you lease or buy, when you do the deal, whether or not you buy add-ons like rustproofing and extended warranties (usually unnecessary with a lease), and the condition of the car you bought when you try to sell it.

The condition of the car can be a real kick in the head. Although most people think their cars are wonderful, most cars are average and average is not so hot.

In terms of pure dollars and cents, the way to save money in the long run is to buy the car, put very few miles on it, keep it in perfect shape, and then sell it yourself for something close to dealer's retail price.

But dollars and cents are never pure.

First, there are the benefits I mentioned earlier: more available cash or credit, and/or driving a nicer car. These are real, solid benefits, and they are worth money. The amount varies, of course, from person to person. Consider them in light of your own circumstances.

Second, selling a car involves work. It can be a lot of work, maybe a lot more than you really want to do.

And don't be too quick to say, "Nah, I can handle it." Keeping a car in good shape takes considerable time and effort, and so does selling it. If you are a person who normally trades in your old car, selling a car probably does involve more work than you really want to do.

Remember, if you drive average miles, your car will have over 50,000 miles on it after four years. That's a lot of wear and tear. And although sellers tend to overlook wear and tear on their cars, prospective buyers tend to notice it.

Some Long-Term Cost Comparisons

Let's take a couple of cars as examples and see how to work out the difference in long-term cost between a buy and a lease.

First, we'll go with a relatively low-priced car. It may as well be the best-selling car in the world at the time of this writing, a Ford Escort.

The sticker price is $8,419. It doesn't have air conditioning, but it's a nice car: a two-door automatic with cloth seats, power steering and brakes, AM/FM four-speaker stereo, power mirrors, body side moldings, and lots of other nice little extras.

We'll assume that you can buy or lease the car for a price of $8,000, including the $10 to $30 the dealer charges for the inspection fee, titling fee, or other minor additional charges.

How big a discount is $419? The car's window sticker shows

an MSRP of $9,126, minus a Ford "options package discount" (for selecting a bunch of options in a group) of $707. This leaves a sticker price of $8,419. At $8,419, the markup on the car would be between $700 and $750.

The dealer, however, will "pack" the car with at least $100. The "pack" or "pac" is an amount of $100 to $200 that the owner adds to the invoice cost for so-called "overhead." As you would expect, the owner and his managers regard the pack as truly part of a car's cost, so the markup shrinks. Our Escort is left with $650 or so "effective" or "after-pack" markup. Thus, since $8,419 includes $650 profit, a discount of $419 (plus the additional charges not charged for, say $10) gives us a deal at $231 over dealer cost ("$231 over"). This is not the best possible deal, perhaps, but it's a good one.

Sales tax varies from place to place. In the Buffalo area it was 8%; around Philly, where I am now, it's 6%, so I'll use 6%. (Incidentally, the higher the tax rate the more you save by leasing.) At 6%, tax on the buy at $8,000 will be $480. Let's assume we put no money down and finance the whole shot: $8,480.

At the moment I write, dealers are quoting interest rates of 11% for a buy and 9% for a lease. You can, however, get financing for 10.5%, so I'll use that as the buy rate and 9.5% as the lease rate. Here, I'm stacking the deck slightly in favor of the buy. For unless a manufacturer is offering lower-than-market interest rates, nominal lease rates usually run a point and a half below the buy rate.

If you buy the car with a four-year loan for $8,480 at 10.5%, your payment will be about $217.50 a month.

If you lease the car early in the year (say January) for 48 months at 9.5% with an $8,000 sell price, your lease payment, derived from Ford Credit lease charts, will be $157.56 plus a 6% tax, on each payment, of $9.45. Your total monthly payment would be $167.01. After 48 buy payments you'd have put out $10,440. After 48 lease payments you'd have put out $8,016. Thus, the lease would save you a total of $2,422, or about fifty bucks each month.

If you buy the car, pay off the loan, then sell the car or trade it in, what will it be worth? Nobody knows.

Ford Credit's official estimate of the car's lease-end or residual value after four years is 32% of the $9,126 MSRP before options discount, or $2,920.

But—you've seen four-year-old Escorts in medium shape on dealers' lots for, say, $3,299. And you figure, "Hell, mine will be worth at least three thousand." You figure you can buy the car and then trade it in—or sell it yourself—and get at least $3,000. You subtract $3,000 from your payout of $10,440, leaving $7,440. Since the payout on the lease was $8,016, you decide that buying and reselling the Escort will save you almost $600!

Uh-unh. If you trade it in, you'll get from $1,700 to $1,900, if that, in "hard dollars." Judging by today, which is all we can do, $1,700 to $1,900 will be the wholesale value of your car. It's what you'd get if you had to turn the car into cash at an auction, which is where the *actual cash value* of automobiles is determined. And it is what you'd get if you traded it in. The "trade allowance" your salesperson tells you about may be higher than the car's cash value, but the overage consists of what are called "show dollars": the discount off the retail price of the new car.

But suppose you sell the car yourself? Won't you get a lot more? You'll get more, but not as much as you may think.

The cars like yours on the dealers' lots for $3,299 have been marked up from the $1,700 to $1,900 the dealer paid for them. The markup includes additional costs, such as overhead, inspection, repair and cleanup work, the price of the warranty, and sales commissions. It also includes discountable money.

Remember, dealers base their prices on the assumption that everybody demands a discount. If a customer walks through the door and smiles, the store will knock off two or three hundred dollars. So the dealer's easy price for the four-year-old Escort would be $3,000. She'd sell it for that in the blink of an eye. The salesperson might put up a struggle, but only to make the customer think he or she was getting a good deal.

So the dealer's retail value for this car would be around

$3,000. Thus, a few hundred dollars under almost any asking price, there is a price that will still put a smile on the dealer's face and joy in the dealer's belly.

If this same smiling customer walks through the door and then negotiates hard, however, the dealer will probably sell that $3,299 four-year-old Escort for, say, $2,750. And this would *not* be a "super" deal for the customer.

That $2,750 covers: the state-mandated Lemon Law warranty (if the state mandates one), the replacement of bald tires, a state inspection, an oil change (if you remember to ask), a fill-up of the antifreeze and squirter fluid, replacement or reattachment of body side moldings, replacement of missing knobs and levers, a steam cleaning of the engine, an interior vacuuming and shampoo, a wash and wax, etc.

If you don't do much of that to your car, as you probably won't, you won't get the money for it, either. So what's your car worth? Twenty-five? Twenty-four? Twenty-three? About that. Three to five hundred less than the dealer's. It's worth about what you've saved through the lower payments on the lease.

Additional Considerations

To illustrate some of the factors that may come into play, let's say you're a very good salesperson and get $2,700 for the average four-plus-year-old Escort. That's a lot: about $900 over wholesale.

Now you've put out $10,440 and recouped $2,700 for a net expense of $7,740. Since you would have spent $8,016 in lease payments, buying and reselling the Escort has, on the face of it, saved you $276 over leasing the car.

However, if you deposit your monthly savings in the bank you'll earn $250 to $400 in interest on the money you've saved by leasing. If you did that, the long-term cost of leasing would be the same or less than that of buying and reselling.

Notice that I haven't subtracted the $40 to $50 in interest you'll lose on the $175 security deposit required on the leased car. But neither have I subtracted the $40 to $200 it will cost to sell the bought car: for the newspaper ad, the wax, the tune-up, a little repair here and there, and the $10 to $50 a week you'll spend to keep the bought car registered and insured while trying to sell it. These selling costs will probably exceed the interest lost on the security deposit, even if the deposit is $400 to $500. In fact, selling costs may consume any savings realized by buying and reselling. Keep them in mind.

Here's another alternative, the one everyone hopes will happen to them. Suppose your Escort is much better than average, a very good one, indeed, and you pick up $3,100 for it. Your net expense on the buy and resale becomes $7,340 (plus selling costs), a significant savings over $8,016. Now the numbers favor buying and reselling . . .

- Unless you paid $500 for rustproofing and paintguard to keep the car nice and spent much more than average in maintenance so you could get that $3,100.
- Or unless you had negotiated a reasonable buyout on the lease for that super-nice Escort. If your lease-end buyout were around $2,600, you could take the $3,100, pay off the lease, and pocket $500 profit (less selling costs, of course). The net expense of leasing would then drop to $7,516.

And, finally, it's quite possible that your four-plus-year-old Escort would be a little ratty, worth no more than $2,100 retail.

Buy		Lease	
Total Payments	$10,440	Total payments	$8,016
Sell for	− 2,100	They clip you for a	
Total cost	$ 8,340	tear in the seat	+ 100
		Total cost	$8,116

In this case, even if you had to give up a chunk of your security deposit, leasing would save you money.

You're probably getting the picture. Circumstances—primarily the value of used cars—vary too greatly for there to be an ironclad rule. But if you keep the car four years, drive an average number of miles, and take moderate care of the car, the long-term costs of a buy and a lease on a new car worth $6,000 to $12,000 are pretty much a wash. This will be true even if you sell the car yourself and get a decent price for it.

As long as you know how to lease right, you will not lose much, if anything, on long-term costs. And the more "average" your car is, the more likely you are to save.

To figure out long-term costs in light of your own circumstances, take into account how many miles you drive, how well you take care of your car, and how you dispose of your cars.

Try to be objective about your car-care habits and realistic about how you dispose of cars. Many people take good care of a car for the first year or so, then slack off. And many people say to themselves, "Oh, I'll sell it for a good price," then end up trading it in.

If you do trade in your car, you will be paid the wholesale price. And leasing right will in most cases save you money.

At this point, many people say, "But I won't have anything after four years."

One thing you won't have is the time and work spent cleaning up and selling your car. With a little bad luck, that time and work can be a major pain in the neck.

One thing you will have is $40 to $120 a month (depending on the cost of the car and the length of the lease) and what that money will earn in interest.

Even if you spend the money and it earns zip, you will not have precisely "nothing." You may have had years of pleasure from the new computer, VCR, or washer and dryer you spent the money on.

How About a More Expensive Car? Say, a Sixteen-five T-Bird?

Assume this Thunderbird's sticker price is $16,500 and its MSRP before the Ford package discount is $17,000. At $16,500, after the discount, around $2,000 effective (after pack) markup will remain on the car. So let's further assume we negotiate a $1,500 store discount to reach a buy or lease price of $15,000.

On a buy, sales tax is paid up front, so we'll add 6% for the tax and come to $15,900. We'll put no money down and finance the whole thing. The payments for a forty-eight-month loan of $15,900 at 10.5% will be about $408 a month.

I say "about" because a mortgage payment book will show a monthly payment of $407.20 a month, while the rate charts from the East Babbit Ford Store will yield $408.63. Quite a difference, huh? Our charts sweetened the juice.

At $408 a month, you will put out $19,584 after four years. Leasing the Bird for four years—based on the $15,000 price and Ford Credit charts—will cost $290.22 plus 6% tax or $307.63 a month. Total four-year outlay will be $14,766.24.

Savings on the lease will be $100.37 a month, or $4,817 over the four years.

Interestingly enough, your savings will be approximately equal to the car's wholesale value if it's—guess what?—average. Wholesale on an average four-year-old Bird carrying the equipment the sixteen-five Bird would carry is around $4,800.

How much can you expect if you sell the car yourself? Well, we occasionally sold *three*-year-old Birds for $6,500. So if your car is decent, you can expect to recover about $5,500 to $6,000.

As we move into larger dollar amounts, it pays to keep in mind inflation and the declining value of money over time. With inflation running at 4% to 5%, as it tends to do, $1,000 in your hand after four years will be worth about $840 in comparison to the thousand you saved in the first ten months of the lease.

Also, bear in mind possible interest earnings on your savings of $100 a month. If you have an average money market checking account earning 6%, your $100 a month deposits will earn you $600 over the four years. Your lease savings will rise to $5,417. If you have a better-than-average account earning 8% (the top 10 earned 8.2% to 8.5% during 1988) your interest earnings would be $835—and total lease savings would be $5,635.

Again, I'll assume a good selling price for the T-Bird: $5,750. If you earned 6% interest on your monthly lease savings, and sell the Bird for $5,750, buying and reselling would save you $332. If you earned 8% on your lease payment savings, buying and reselling would save you $97.

Total lease payments:	$14,766	Total buy payments:	$19,584
Interest earned	− 600	Sale price:	− 5,750
Net expense	$14,166	Net expense	$13,834
Interest at 8%	− 235	Plus selling costs: ads,	
Net expense	$13,931	tune-up, repairs, etc.	?

The $97 savings will be reduced by selling costs.

You may think that a four-year-old car in this class will bring more than $5,750. Ford, however, estimates the residual at 34% of $17,000 or $5,780. That $5,780 would be the lease-end buyout. As I've mentioned, unless you negotiate it, your buyout will be set at a fat retail price. The wholesale residual value underlying this lease payment is about $4,800.

Now I am not subtracting taxes from your interest earnings. You may or may not have to pay them. Neither am I subtracting the loss of value due to inflation from the money you make selling the Bird. Losses to the IRS on the lease deal will probably be matched or exceeded by losses to inflation on the buy, and, if not, then by additional losses due to selling costs.

After selling costs, net savings realized by buying and reselling the Thunderbird at $5,750 would be somewhere between $0 and $200. This higher end is enough to notice, but not, I believe, enough to worry about. And if you consider the $0 to

$200 as interest paid later to have an extra $1,200 per year over a four-year period, even the high end is next to nothing.

As before, individual circumstances vary so much that no absolute pronouncements are possible.

- Your car might be worth $7,000. This is highly unlikely, but should it happen, you could sell the car, pay off the lease, and take the overage. In our example here, the unnegotiated lease-end buyout would be $5,780.
- Another possibility, and a very real one: Your Bird may be worth $5,000 or less. If you bought and resold, you'd lose money.
- And, finally, if you bought and then traded in, you'd almost certainly lose money, no matter how nice the car.

Once again, on average, the long-term cost of leasing differs little from that of buying and reselling.

NOTE: To calculate buy payments, buy a loan payment book that includes tables for short-term (two- to six-year) loans. They cost only $5 to $10 dollars. Then buy a $5 to $10 pocket calculator. Look up the cost of a thousand-dollar loan at the appropriate percentage rate and term. This gives you cost per thousand. Then put a decimal point and a zero in front of that number and round it off to five digits. Now you have the factor for that term and interest rate, e.g., payment on $1,000 borrowed for four years at 10.5% is $25.61. Thus, the 10.5% 48-month factor is .02561. To calculate your payment, multiply the amount you are borrowing by the factor.

Long-Term Costs of a Five-Year Lease vs. a Five-Year Buy

Interest rates on 60-month loans usually run half a point to a point higher than on 48-month loans. So I'll use 11% for the five-year buy and 10% for the lease.

The Thunderbird: Financing $15,900 for five years at 11% will run you about $346 a month ($345.70 on my financial calculator, $346.62 on my charts from the Ford store). Using $346, after 60 months you will have paid out $20,760.

Leasing the Bird for 60 months will cost $252.50, plus 6% tax, or $267.65 per month. After 60 months you will have paid out $16,059. The lease would save you $4,701, about average *dealer's* retail price on a five-year-old Bird ($900 to $1200 over wholesale). Assuming then that you get dealer's retail for your five-year-old Bird, the long-term costs are a wash. If you don't get that price, you'll save by leasing. The chances are that you won't get that price.

Many people buy cars on five-year loans. They don't do it because they want to keep the car for five years, they do it to get affordable payments.

The figures do not usually support that decision.

Some people, however, believe that they can buy with a five-year loan, then sell or trade after four years, thereby saving more money than they would by leasing. What these folks often forget is that loans are heavily front-loaded. This means that you pay a much greater proportion of the interest in the beginning of the loan than you do in the end. And, conversely, you pay a much greater proportion of the principal at the end. Result? After making a lot of payments, you have paid less principal, and owe more, than you thought.

Leasing for Four Years Compared to Buying for Five and Selling After Four

The Thunderbird's four-year lease payment was $307.63, including tax. Total expense: $14,766.

Instead of leasing, suppose you take out a five-year buy loan and sell the car after four years. Your monthly payment is $346. After making 48 payments, you've paid $16,608 (48 × $346). Your remaining balance is $3,911. You must pay it off. $16,608 plus $3,911 = $20,519. If you sell the car for $5,750, you're left with a net expense of $14,769. You lose three dollars.

Trade the car in—as many people do—and you lose about a thousand dollars more.

On the Escort—in fact, on most cars—the figures would be, relatively speaking, the same.

Assuming your credit is good enough to lease, buying on a five-year loan is probably not the best way to go. If the lowest possible payment is your goal, a five-year lease will meet it. If you are flexible as to payments, those of a four-year lease tend to be about the same as those of a five-year buy. And you are out of the car after four years—without having to come up with cash out of pocket to pay off the balance on the loan. Neither do you have to keep paying through that fifth year for a car that may have become a little less than wonderful.

Exception: If you drive very few miles and keep your car in excellent shape, things change. Leasing loses some of its reason for being. Most lease programs base their payments on the expectation that the car will be driven about 15,000 miles a year. Lease a car that you'll drive 4,000 miles a year, and you pay for mileage you will not use.

NOTE: Your lender may charge lease rates different from those above. Or rates may have changed nationwide. You cannot use the figures here except as examples with which to practice and to understand how to make the comparison. So, too, with the values of the used cars. You may live in a market where everybody wants the car I'm discussing, thus inflating its price. Or where nobody wants that particular car, drastically reducing its price. You must discover the details that pertain to your locality.

SHOULD YOU PUT DOWN CASH TO GET LOW PAYMENTS ON A BUY?

One frequently sees advice to the effect that you should put as much cash down on a car as you can afford. Then buy it by taking the shortest loan whose payments you can afford. By doing so, you are supposed to save money on interest charges.

My feeling is that if you have tons of money, maybe you should do this. However, if you don't have tons of money, you probably shouldn't. How do you decide?

First, answer a question: Where will the cash down come from? If it will come from a bank, it should be earning interest for you. The next question is, will your savings in unpaid interest be more than your earnings in interest on the cash left sitting in the bank? Here's how to figure it out.

We'll compare a buy with cash down to one with nothing down, then a buy with cash down to a lease with nothing down.

Buy with Cash Down vs. Buy with Nothing Down

Let's use the Escort, on which we were financing $8,480. We'll assume you're not too happy with that $217.50 monthly payment, so you decide to put down $2,000.

If you put down $2,000 and pay off $6,480 at 10.5% over four years, you'll pay $166.20 a month.

> Total monthly payments with no cash down: $217.50 × 48 = $10,440
> Total monthly payments with $2,000 down: $166.20 × 48 = $7,977.60
> Savings: $10,440 − $7,977.60 = $2,462.40, or $2,462

Over the life of the loan, you pay out $2,462 less. In other words, putting down $2,000 saved you $462 in interest.

On the other hand, if that $2,000 sits in a passbook savings account for four years at 5.5% (according to *Money* magazine the national average at the time of writing) it will earn $492 in interest. Your $2,000 in the bank earns more than it saves when put down on the car. You end up with an extra $30. And, more important, you have the $2,000 available should you happen to need it.

Now, if that $2,000 sits in an 8% certificate of deposit (CD) for four years, it will earn $751 in interest. You'll be almost $300 ahead of the game, and, again, the cash will be available for emergencies.

How can this be? Because the amount you are being charged interest on is declining, while the amount you are earning interest on is increasing.

Another way to calculate the total savings a downstroke (down payment) will provide is to compute the payment with it and without it, then subtract the smaller payment from the larger. Then multiply the difference by the number of months in the loan.

$$\$217.50 - \$166.20 = \$51.30$$
$$\$51.30 \times 48 = \$2,462.40$$

To find out how much interest your proposed down payment will earn, simply call a local bank. Pick one that pays interest compounded monthly. Ask how much you'll have after four years if you deposit that amount in their 48-month CD.

Buy with Cash Down vs. Lease with Nothing Down

Here's the buy with $2,000 down compared to the lease with nothing down.

Four-Year Buy, $2,000 Down		Four-Year Lease, Nothing Down	
Monthly payment	$ 166.20	Monthly payment	$ 167.01
Lease term	× 48	Lease term	× 48
Total	$7,977.60	Total	$8,016.48
Cash down	+ 2,000.00	Less 8% interest on	
Total	9,977.60	$2,000 in CD	− 751.00
Less resale	− 2,700.00	Net expense	$7,265.48
Net expense	$7,277.60		

Again, you may be taxed on your interest earnings; you may spend a couple hundred to sell the car; the car may be worth much less than $2,700.

Assuming that these "maybes" will more or less cancel one another out, the lease beats the buy. Total expense is about the same. But the lease leaves you in possession of the $2,000. Put it down on the car and it won't be there, should you happen to need it in an emergency.

A point I haven't mentioned is that there are investments that earn more than 8%. I use CD's and asset management accounts as examples because they are insured and thus, barring disaster, safe. But you may find a higher-yielding investment that has the degree of safety you want (e.g., bond funds, which with little risk returned 14% in 1988).

A RULE OF THUMB

If you can invest at a rate reasonably close to the rate you will be charged for the car loan, it makes no sense to put money down. By close, I mean something like the spread we saw in our examples, where financing costs (interest you pay) were 10% to 11%, and earnings ran from 5.5% to 8% on safe and readily available investments. Thus, interest costs on financing were four and a half to five points higher than interest earnings on a passbook savings account, and two to three points higher than earnings on a CD.

In terms of dollar amounts (whether you are considering a down payment on an installment loan, or a down payment on a lease), if investing the money will earn more in interest than putting it down on the car will save, or if those earnings equal the savings, or if earnings are only a little lower than savings, keep your cash.

SHOULD YOU BUY FOR CASH?

Some folks dream of being able to pay cash for a car. Being *able* to do so is great, but how good is actually *doing* it? Let's compare the expense of buying for cash to the expense of leasing.

Suppose you buy the Thunderbird (or similar car) for $15,900 cash. You drive it for four years, then recoup $5,800 by selling it. How do you make out?

SCENARIO 1

$15,900 − $5,800 = $10,100 (net expense)
$307.63 (lease payment) × 48 = $14,766

But instead of paying $15,900 for the car, you kept it in an 8% CD compounded monthly—and earned $5,973 in interest.

$14,766 − $5,973 = $8,793 (net expense)

Leasing saved you $1,307.

SCENARIO 2

You pay cash. Since you are not making lease payments you have an extra $307.63 available each month. You take it out of your income and put it in the bank.

After 48 months you have deposited $14,766. If you earn a constant 5.5% you'll end up with $16,474. You've earned $1,708 in interest.

$10,100 − $1,708 = $8,392 (net expense)
$8,793 − $8,392 = $401.

Buying for cash saved you $401. (Not if you traded in, however, or got less than $5,800 for the Bird.)

SCENARIO 3

You are unhappy. You hate to lose $401, even though it is zip to pay for control over $15,900 for 48 months, for the lease permitted you to retain control of almost $16,000 cash for four years at a cost of $400. Suppose an opportunity came along to earn 20% on that money? Nevertheless, it galls you to lose $401. What do you do?

Shop for a lower lease payment by finding a lender who ascribes a higher residual value to Thunderbirds.

Say, for example, you locate a dealer or lease store that can put the deal through a bank which ascribes a 36% residual value to the Bird, instead of Ford's 34%. Assume the purchase price of the car is raised ("bumped") $200 to cover a bank fee. Even so, because of the higher residual value, your payment will come down to $296.56, including 6% tax.

Multiply $296.56 by 48 to get the total payout of $14,235. Subtracting the $5,973 in interest earned leaves a net expense of $8,262, compared to the $8,392 of buying for cash. Leasing lets you keep the cash and saves you $130.

One other thing you should be aware of.

Cash will not get you a better deal at the car store. When you are financed through Friendly First National, Friendly First pays cash to the dealer, and then collects from you. To the dealer, all deals are cash.

THE SECURITY DEPOSIT: HOW MUCH? IS IT NEGOTIABLE?

The refundable security deposit secures the lessor against damage or excessive wear and tear to the car.

On both Ford and GMAC leases, the amount deposited has traditionally been the amount of the payment rounded upward to the nearest multiple of 25. With a lease payment of $143, your security deposit would be $150. A payment of $156.89 results in a security deposit of $175. Payment of $378 brings a deposit of $400.

Some lessors ask for higher deposits: payment plus $100, payment plus $200, or a flat $400.

The deposit is refundable, but having to put out so much cash cuts into the advantage you seek from leasing in the first place.

The amount may be negotiable, and it's worth a try, but don't count on it. Instead, go after a lower payment.

Suppose you've made a deal for price and payment, then find out the lender wants a big security deposit. Tell the salesperson that GM and Ford require deposits of payment rounded to the next highest multiple of 25. So if you have to put out a higher security deposit, you want a lower payment. Suppose the amount is $100 more than GMAC requires. Over four years, you'll lose about $40 in interest. So on a 48-month lease, the payment should drop $1 a month. Right?

By the way, should you prefer not to put out cash, the dealer should be able to get the security deposit financed.

Consider this. If the lease rate is low, it may be worth doing. The lower the lease rate, the more worth doing it is. To decide, find out how much higher your lease payment will be. Multiply that overage by the number of payments. Take the resulting total and subtract the amount of the deposit. The remainder will be what you have to pay in finance charges.

CAN I TRADE IN MY OLD CAR WHEN I LEASE A NEW ONE?

As salesmen like to say, No-o-o-o problem.

Whatever your car is worth beyond what you owe on it (your equity) will be deducted from the acquisition cost of the leased car.

To put it another way, the trade equity will be deducted from the amount you finance on the lease. In the Escort example, if you traded in a car worth $2,000 that you owned free and clear, your payment would drop to $112.06, tax included. (You would save $637 in interest charges, while losing $751 in interest earnings.)

CAN YOU TRADE IN A LEASED CAR?

No-o-o-o problem. Just like a buy. If the car is worth more than the payoff on the lease, that's your equity. It's credited against the new lease just like a cash down payment.

CAN YOU TAKE YOUR EQUITY IN CASH?

In all probability, yes. If your credit is good and you want your trade equity in cash, most dealers will hand you a check.

Two Views of Equity in Cash

1. If you can make the payment, take the cash. Consider it in the light of our discussion of cash down payments.

2. However, paying cash for your equity can be used as a pressure tactic, a way to push you into dealing fast, dealing now, with no further negotiation. For instance: "I can put you in the Glitzmobile for $265.27 a month, right now, today, and cut you a check for six hundred and ninety-five dollars. You can drive home in a brand-new car with seven hundred dollars in your pocket."

If you hear something like this before you have agreed on the deal you want, you should ignore the vision of greenbacks dancing in your head.

CAN YOU TRADE IN A (LEASED OR OTHER) CAR WITH NEGATIVE EQUITY?

You sure can. Your negative equity (the amount you owe beyond what your car is worth) is simply added to the price of the new car and you pay it off with your monthly payments. You can do this on a lease or a buy.

Most banks, however, will not want your paper if you do.

But the factory credit companies are another story. They won't mind—as long as your credit is good and the amount of your negative equity does not push the balance on the new car too, too far beyond its value.

This is an important point to remember. In many situations, the manufacturer's credit arms will put a higher priority on selling the manufacturer's car than on making a perfectly sensible loan, the way a bank would. This can help you escape from an unreliable used car for which you owe more than you can get. But it can also help you bury yourself forever in the new car.

CAN YOU HAVE NEGATIVE EQUITY AFTER YOU'VE MADE THE LEASE PAYMENTS FOR THE FULL TERM?

No, you cannot. With two exceptions.

1. You bring the car back damaged. As noted earlier, it's your responsibility to pay for repairs. If somebody hits your car with a hammer, spend the insurance check to fix it.

2. You made the mistake of signing an open-end lease. Some of these can sound good. "Look at this," the salesperson tells you. "You can collect the profit when the lease expires. If it's worth more than we thought it would be, we'll pay you the difference. You could really make out."

Sure you could. This is a lousy gamble. There's only a slight chance that the car will be worth more than the original estimate when you turn it in. And there's a very good chance that it will be worth less than the original estimate. If less, you pay the difference.

I WANT TO OWN MY CAR AND KEEP IT FOREVER. CAN LEASING HELP ME IN ANY WAY?

Yes, because leasing will put you into more car for a lower payment. You could then treat the lease as a buy with an extended term. When the lease expired, you could finance the buyout for two or three more years.

Obviously, this means higher interest charges and more money out of pocket in the long run. But the lower payment could make it possible for you to have a car that suited your needs rather than a car that you could afford.

WHAT HAPPENS IF THE CAR IS STOLEN OR DESTROYED?

There are snares and pitfalls in everything, right?

Right. One of them is the problem of forced early termination.

This can be a big problem when you buy. When you lease, however, it can be bigger. The slower payoff of a lease loan, combined with the lessor's attempts to impose penalties and to recover all or part of the car's residual value, aggravates the situation.

If your car were stolen and never recovered or totaled in an accident early on in the lease, your insurance check could fall thousands of dollars short of what you owe.

During the first few months you have your car, it will drop in value by the amount of all the dealer charges, including finance and advertising charges, freight and so on, over its cost—plus its depreciation for time and wear. Thus, in a few short months your car will depreciate 25% to 30%.

Clearly, your payments will not cover this loss in value.

As the months go by, the amount you have to pay to make up the difference will not necessarily go down. Whether you buy or lease, the car may continue to depreciate faster than you are paying it off. But the lower lease payment makes the difference between what your car is worth and what you owe even greater.

Should the car be destroyed or stolen, the sum you were obligated to pay could be painfully large.

Ways Around the Problem

"*Gap insurance*" Gap insurance insures you against the auto insurer's settlement falling short of the balance owed to the lender—it covers the gap. In late '89, gap insurance costs approximately 1.5% of the monthly lease payment. On a payment of $200 a month, the total premium would be $144. You can pay it up front or in monthly installments.

This premium reduces your savings through leasing—and eliminates the risk of losing thousands, a risk you run whether you lease or buy on time.

A *Deal with No Additional Charges* Even if you cannot make a deal for an early *voluntary* buyout without penalties, shop for, negotiate for, and push hard for a deal where you pay no penalties and no part of the residual value, nor any other extra costs if early termination is forced upon you by theft or accidental disaster.

Such deals can be had. In the Philadelphia area, for example, one of the larger lease stores promises that the banks it uses will collect only the balance of their purchase costs should the car be a total loss. If one store can persuade its lenders to do that, so can others. You would, of course, be sure to get that promise in writing, in the lease contract itself or in a rider that is explicitly identified in the contract.

Changing the Contract If your lease contract specifies prepayment penalties in the event of involuntary termination, negotiate with the salesperson to get that clause crossed out and a new one, charging no prepayment penalties and no part of the residual value, written in.

The salesman and manager shouldn't give you a hard time about this. All they have to do is call the credit company and ask if the lease will be accepted if it's changed the way you want.

If the lessor is the manufacturer's credit company, it will

probably accept the changed contract. With a bank, the result is harder to predict.

If the lender balks, the dealership's finance guy or manager can try persuasion. (This is often done and often works.) Or he can try to find another lender who will accept the lease the way you want it.

Provisions Already in the Lease Some lease contracts do not require payment of the balance owed. Instead, they require that the lost car be replaced by a substitute.

Chrysler Credit Corporation's contract, for example, requires you to accept a replacement vehicle, to be provided by Chrysler credit or the original vehicle's insurer. If you refuse to accept the replacement, you are in default on the contract.

Ford leases have a somewhat similar provision, but offer less protection. A Ford Credit lease makes it your responsibility to provide the replacement vehicle. You go out with insurance money in hand and buy a used car for Ford Credit.

It's amusing to think of you, or me for that matter, out there waving a rather puny insurance check and trying to buy a used car for Ford Motor Company: a company that has access to thousands of used cars at wholesale and ten billion dollars in cash, to boot.

If you are currently in a contract that requires you to provide the replacement vehicle, don't worry too much. Should the car be destroyed, go to the dealer or lease store. Try to talk them into finding, helping you find, or persuading the lessor to find the replacement vehicle. It will be easier for them than for you, and most of them will do it. They want repeat business.

In case you prefer not to buy Ford Credit a replacement car, the lease provides an alternative. You can pay off a balance calculated according to a very badly expressed formula contained in a very clotted and very confusing paragraph, Paragraph 21. The only thing in it easy to understand is that Ford wants an early termination fee of $200.

Your dealer should be willing to try to talk Ford Credit out of that fee; your dealer may well be, and probably will be, willing to try to talk them into accepting the balance of the purchase price as the payoff.

GMAC lease contracts used to offer the least protection of the big three. Now, to become competitive, they are more or less the same. In case of a total loss, you may pay off the balance owed specified by the early termination clause we discussed previously. Or "if you and the Lessor agree in writing you may continue [the] lease with a substitute vehicle." GMAC's contracts used to say "at Lessor's election" you may substitute a vehicle. It's still at the lessor's election, for the lessor has to agree with you in writing, but the language now makes GMAC sound a bit more willing to do so.

Now as then, however, the language obscures responsibility for providing the vehicle. Who? You or them?

This could give you a few sleepless nights should your car take a trip to the local chop shop. But, again, your dealer should be willing to work with you to persuade GMAC to be as reasonable as possible.

The best time for your dealer or lease store to work with you is not after disaster strikes but when you do the deal.

Certain paragraphs in lease contracts are written so that most people will have a very hard time understanding what they mean. Have any such paragraphs explained thoroughly and, if necessary, changed. And make sure the explanation is precise. I can easily imagine a salesman saying, "Oh, it's like when you jump off a roof. You wouldn't jump off a roof, would you? Then don't worry about it." I kid you not.

Once you are sure the explanation actually explains what the paragraph means, have either the explanation or the changes you want written into the contract before you sign it. Or, for that matter, even after you sign it—as long as you have not taken delivery of the car. Never forget: no matter how many times a car store manager says, "You bought it, pal," you have not bought the deal and you are not stuck with the car until you drive it off the lot. Until then, you can always demand your deposit back, get it back, and go home.

The changes to seek in the event of involuntary early termination are

- That the lessor, lease store, or dealer accepts responsibility to provide a replacement car. It won't be a new car, by the way. It's age and condition will be similar to yours. You may not like it as much as yours; you may like it more.
- That if you are not at fault, you have the option to pay off the balance of the purchase price in lieu of supplying a replacement car. Push hard for these changes. You should not be penalized for something over which you have no control.

Most cars, of course, are not stolen or destroyed. So . . .

WHAT DO YOU DO WHEN THE LEASE IS UP?

You bring the car back to the dealer or lease store you got it from, then buy it or give it back. If you give it back, the store then either sells it, or arranges to return it to the lender/lessor.

The car you bring back is supposed to be in average condition for its age. If not, you forfeit whatever part of your security deposit is needed to bring it into average condition. And more, if it takes more.

At the place I worked, and I think at most car stores, average means average. Normally, a dealer will not be as harsh a judge of the condition of your car as would, say, a bank: The dealer wants to lease you another car, not have you stomp off the lot swearing at him over a couple hundred dollars.

- The car should have tires that will pass inspection (sometimes expressed as tread 1/8 inch deep).
- The light bulbs should all be there and working, as should the radio that came with the car, and everything else that came

with the car. You are not supposed to take the jack and the spare as going-away presents to yourself.

- The sheet metal is not supposed to be bent, folded, or mutilated. Nicks and dings are generally okay. But if you smack the car, you are supposed to spend your insurance check to get it fixed, not to finance a trip to Aruba. If you drill holes in the car, you will have to pay to have them filled.
- The exhaust system is supposed to be on the car, not completely rotted out.
- The window glass is not supposed to be cracked or smashed.

"Average condition" is pretty much a matter of common sense. It's not perfect. Neither is it smashed up or with parts missing. But read your lease contract carefully before signing it. Make sure it contains no zingers about the condition of the car. Here are some that could cost you hundreds of dollars:

- New or "good" tires as opposed to inspectable tires.
- "Good retail condition" instead of average condition. Good retail condition could be interpreted as "clean," and the difference between "average" and "clean" starts at about $500 and goes to $2,000 or more.
- No body rust permitted in an area of the country where rust is common, if not inevitable.
- A requirement that you pay to repair faulty power window mechanisms and other electronic malfunctions. Watch out for this. It strongly suggests that the lessor expects the power doodads to break shortly after the warranty expires. Power doodads are very expensive to repair.

There may be others. Check carefully.

THREE

Getting Ready

There are a few things to learn and a few decisions to make before you go out to do a deal.

- How leasing might influence your choice of car
- How to determine dealer cost
- What is a good deal
- What to do with your present car
- How to price your present car
- When to do a lease deal
- Where to do the deal
- How to calculate lease payments
- How to understand advertisements

WHICH CAR IS THE CAR FOR YOU?

The one you like. The car for you is the car that rings your bell.

I mean, be a little reasonable. Don't get a Corvette if you've got a wife, a husband, four kids, and a dog and you spend a lot of time hauling firewood. And do look up the repair records in a consumer publication. The principal way some manufacturers cut costs on some of their cars is to cut the weight, strength, and ruggedness of parts.

Then, if its breakdown record is more or less average, go with the car that steals your heart. Or the one that fits your family.

Leasing may affect your decision because two very similar cars can have very different payments. In the case of two cars priced approximately the same, the one with the higher residual value will cost you less per month. And, therefore, cost less overall, unless you buy it at the end of the term.

In fact, if the residuals differ sufficiently, you can pay less for a more expensive car.

Let's suppose you were deciding between a Ford Taurus and a Chevy Celebrity. At the time of this writing, the Taurus has a little more equipment, because Ford makes more stuff standard and puts a little more in comparable packages. It retails for $14,900. The Celebrity has a little less equipment and retails for $14,550. Let's say you can lease the Ford based on a price of $13,450; the Chevy for $13,100.

When I look up a major Pennsylvania bank's 48-month residual values for the two cars, I find the Celebrity's residual is 33% and the Taurus's is 36% (of "retail" or "sticker" price, because we'll assume no option package discount).

Assuming no package discounts, then, and a 10% lease rate, you pay (before tax) $246.86 per month for the Taurus, and $247.49 for the Celebrity. The Taurus has bigger, wider tires, which provide better handling, a bigger engine, and a power driver seat. You pay less and get more because the lender considers the Taurus to have a higher residual value.

If two or three different vehicles are equally suitable for you—and you are not interested in buying out the lease—compare the residual values. Go with the highest residual and, everything else being equal, you will get more car for the same or less money.

DETERMINING DEALER COSTS

Knowing these numbers may help you decide between cars. And they supply a vantage point that will help you understand everything else. Dealer cost is like a mark on a map to show where your house is when you move into a strange neighborhood.

Buy a copy of a new car price book, like *Edmund's New Car Prices* or Consumer Guide's *Car Specs and Prices* (Publications International, Ltd., 3841 W. Oakton St., Skokie, IL, 60076). Both are available at bookstores, newsstands, and often at drugstores and discount stores with big magazine racks.

Make sure the book is current. Not too old—and not too new. The factories raise car prices when they introduce the new year's models, then usually bump (meaning raise or increase) them twice more during the year: at the turn of the calendar year, and in the spring. Obviously, you could get a book that is out of date and does not cover a recent price increase. But since the books come out before the price bumps, you can also get one that's not in date yet, one that shows a price increase not yet in effect.

To check, look on the book's cover. The months for which the book is supposed to be accurate will be printed there. To double-check, take it with you to a car store and compare the retail prices. If they correspond, the book is up-to-date. If the book is consistently low, the price has been bumped and the book is too old. If it's consistently high, the book is too new, and the cars for the period covered have not yet reached the stores.

The latter problem can occur around the time of a price change. When the new books come out, the publisher usually pulls the old ones off the shelves. But if the old books disappear while the cars at dealerships are still old-price cars, you cannot get an accurate readout on their costs.

A solution is available from the Consumers Union, publisher of *Consumer Reports*. For $10 to $15 per car, they'll mail you a cost and price list for any car(s) you specify, along with all available options (256 Washington St., Mount Vernon, N.Y. 10553).

Interpreting the Cost and Price Books

You may have to do a little work to adjust the numbers you find in these books. One thing to watch for is that some books clump together the freight charges for all cars in a section at the back of the book. If you forget to look up the freight back there, your cost and price numbers will be $300 to $500 lower than the actual amounts. Too picky? Well, I forgot to do it, then spent twenty minutes wondering why the lease payment I had just calculated was the best deal the world had ever seen. Freight charges are kept separate by both manufacturer and dealer, but they are a nonnegotiable part of both the car's cost and its price.

Turning to the back of the book isn't much work. You may have to do a bit more when adjusting both retail price and dealer cost figures.

Price

The difficulty with price occurs because of options package discounts (a number of options is grouped together, then tagged as a group with a discounted price). When you buy, package discounts mean little. But when you lease, they mean a lot because cars with them, "package cars" as they are called, have two retail prices, one before and one after the discount.

The price before the discount, which we're calling the MSRP (Manufacturers Suggested Retail Price), is the one used to calculate the car's residual value. The second, which we're calling "sticker price" or "retail," is the retail price of the car as it sits on the lot.

The key to recognizing package cars of any make or model is those two prices on the window sticker. Look for them. The sticker will show the base price for the car, the freight charges, perhaps some options not in the package, then a bunch of options in a group identified with letters or numbers. Then everything will be added up: base price, freight, other options, and the retail price of each option in the package. The sum will be the MSRP. Then, from that number the package discount will be subtracted, and what's left will be the sticker price. Like this:

Spudrovia Fabucar ZZT

Base price	$ 9,000
Freight (sometimes shown at end)	+ 300
Pearly-Glow Paint	+ 200
Options Group 69A	
Option 1	+ 100
Option 2	+ 100
Option 3	+ 100
Option 4	+ 100
Option 5	+ 100
	$10,000
MSRP discount on Option Group 69A	− 100
MSRP ("sticker price")	$ 9,900

The problem is that some consumer cost and price books ignore the package discounts. They treat the options package as an item that has a cost to the dealer—the sum of the dealer costs for the options—and a retail price to you, which corresponds *not* to the sum of the retail prices of the options but to the already discounted price for the package.

A book that uses the already discounted package price to arrive at the price of the car will ignore the MSRP and show only the car's sticker price—$9,900 rather than $10,000 in terms of our example—which is the price after the package discount. If you use that price to calculate residual value, you will end up with a residual that is too low, making the lease payment, supposed to be a good deal for you, too high.

Check your book carefully to see how it handles package discounts. If it doesn't handle them, make sure you do. If the book doesn't mention an MSRP discounted to arrive at the retail price, you will have to visit a car lot and look at a car's window sticker to see if the model you want is a package car.

If you don't, you may end up by selling yourself a bad deal. For example, the Escort we discussed had an MSRP of $9,126, but a sticker price of $8,419, after a package discount of $707. Using $8,419 to calculate residual value would result in a before-tax payment of $161.42 instead of $157.56, a difference of $185.28 over the term of the lease.

Cost and Dealer Cost

Once you have the price, or, since many of today's cars come with packages, two prices, you then need to know the *dealer cost*.

The consumer cost and price books will provide you with the base cost of the car, the costs of all the options and/or packages, and the delivery or freight charges.

Now you have a little more work to do to reach the total cost, for finance charges and advertising fees will be added to the costs just mentioned. If the manufacturer is floorplanning (financing) the dealership, the finance charges will appear on the car's invoice. If a bank is financing the dealership, the finance charges will appear on the dealer's books. Typically, at today's interest rates (mid- to late 1989) finance charges add ³⁄₄ to ⁷⁄₈ of 1% to the cost of the car.

Also part of dealer cost is the dealer contribution to the factory's advertising program, sometimes called the *Dealer Advertising Fee*. Estimate another three quarters of one percent to cover advertising. Some of the new car-cost books investigate these fees, but some do not. If your book does not, add a minimum of 1.5% to the cost to account for them.

Dealer cost, interestingly enough, includes a sum the dealer doesn't pay. When the car is sold and the dealer pays the factory, 3% to 5% is subtracted and either held out of the payment, or kicked back later. That's the holdback: a part of the "cost" that the dealer does not pay the factory.

But you can't get your greedy little hands on it.

For the dealer has it firmly clutched in his own greedy little hands. Owners of dealerships regard the holdback as sacred: theirs by divine right. They don't pay commission on it and they don't go into it in order to give you a better deal.

Finally, the last dealer cost item is the dealer's pack mentioned in Chapter Two: $100 to $200 is added to the cost for so-called "overhead."

The size of the pack depends on the intensity of the competition in the area. Neighboring dealers usually add similar amounts. But unless you know someone in the business, the only way to discover that amount is to ask your salesperson.

Estimate $100 for low-priced cars (below $9,000) and $150 for others. During negotiation, ask. Ask at a point when the salesman is insisting that you pay more than you are offering.

Do not, however, expect the pack to be discounted. Even in the East Babbit–area car shoppers' paradise, with nine almost contiguous Ford dealers tearing at each other's throats, we did not discount down into the pack.

Here's a list of cost items:

Base price for the model (make sure you've got the right number
   of doors; 4-door cars are usually more expensive)
+ Option 1
+ Option 2
+ Option . . . n
+ Freight (also called "destination" and "delivery")
+ Finance charges
+ Dealer Advertising Fee
———————————————————
   "Invoice cost"
+ The pack
———————————————————
   Total
+ Dealer prep (sometimes illegitimate)

If your dealer claims extra cost for prep, complain. The manufacturer includes dealer prep in the invoice. If the dealer tries to charge you for it, he's trying to charge you twice. Go somewhere else.

Additional Charges

At the East Babbit store, we charged an inspection fee, but this was limited to the state fee for the sticker. We also charged a "titling fee" of $10, $3 to New York for the title and $7 more to the dealer for the car.

Our extra charges were low, but we were held in check by the intensity of the competition. If you live in an area where competition is mild, the local dealer may try to hit you for more of these little extras. Object, strenuously. The dealer doesn't need them to make a ton of money. And besides, if they give you a good deal, you're going to lease your next 10 cars from them, right? You sure are. Make sure they know it.

COST TO LEASE STORES

Lease stores buy vehicles from dealerships. Some of them receive a discount known as the "fleet discount" or "fleet incentive."

The amount of this discount varies from manufacturer to manufacturer and from model to model. It can go from zero to $100 off invoice cost to the amount of the finance charges off invoice cost—all the way up to $700 off cost plus a free option or two. Whatever it is, the dealer will tack on a pack of $100 to $200 and a markup of $75 to $100.

When you figure cost to a lease store, you'll have to call dealerships or a factory rep to discover the amount of the fleet discount on the model you want. Then add $150 pack and $100 for dealer profit. This will provide you with a preliminary estimate of the lease store's cost.

Then, when talking to the store's salesperson, you'll need to ask some more questions. Ask about:

- The amount of the fleet discount off standard dealer cost—to make sure the store gets it and, if it does, to see how much of it is being passed on to you.
- The amount of the dealer's pack and profit.
- The lease store's pack and profit.

Even if the store refuses to discuss its pack and profit, once you have cost from a cost book and the amount of the fleet discount you can reach a fairly accurate estimate of the lease store's cost. And from there, of course, calculate the store's profit.

COST OF MINIVANS, UTILITY, AND SPORT VEHICLES

"Utility" and "sport" vehicles are things like Broncos and Bronco II's, Blazers and S-10 Blazers, etc. Although called trucks, cost and price are handled like cars. So too are the cost and price of down-sized pickup trucks and minivans.

The "retail price" of a full-sized truck, pickup, or van may be a little different.

Light Trucks (Pickups and Vans)

For the past five or more years, the highest-selling single nameplate vehicle in the world has been the Ford F-150 pickup truck. As with cars, more of them are being leased every day. The way you cost out a truck and the way you do the deal are exactly the same as with a car.

But the retail price on a truck can be one number today, and another tomorrow, changing at the whim of a salesperson or manager. The full-sized Ford truck—pickup or van—does not have a price on the window sticker. Chevy truck stickers have prices. But at some of the Chevy dealerships I've visited, the trucks don't have stickers.

The federal government, you see, does not force the car companies to put retail prices on trucks. And when a vehicle doesn't wear a factory sticker with a retail price, the dealer sets the price.

This is normally done by taking cost plus pack and then adding 15% or 16% of that figure. If the truck costs the dealer ten grand, he adds a hundred or two for his pack, then adds 15% (sometimes 16%) of that (say, $10,200 with a $200 pack), and comes up with something like $11,730. Plus some pennies, you know, to make it look real.

However, different managers use different percentages. Or the same one will use different percentages at different times.

We had a truck manager for a while who, when he was feeling good, computed retail on a truck by marking it up 25% or 30%. So the price he'd quote on the ten-grand-cost truck with a $200 pack would be $12,750. Plus pennies: $12,750.44.

Some customers howled. Some customers walked out. Some customers took a thousand-dollar discount and thought they got a hell of a deal.

Until recently, you had no way of knowing when this was being done to you. But now Edmund Publications (515 Hempstead Turnpike, West Hempstead, N.Y., 11552) puts out a book of truck costs and prices. If you are going to lease a truck, get that book or one like it. Cost structure is the same as a car's, i.e., base, options, freight, finance charges, advertising, pack, etc. So is price structure, with options packages and package discounts. So, too, then, is the need to find out if the MSRP before discount is higher than the sticker price.

You do lease deals and calculate lease payments on light trucks the same way you do with cars. If, however, you will use the truck commercially, the lender will deduct 5% to 10% from its residual value.

WHAT IS A GOOD DEAL?

How much profit should the dealer make from you? Here are some guidelines.

- On an "inexpensive" car in the Escort class or below, which retails for $9,000 to $10,000 or less: $200 to $250.
- On a retail price of $10,000 to $14,000: $300 to $400.
- $14,000 to $19,000: $400 to $500.
- $19,000 to $23,000: $500 to $600.
- On trucks, same as above.

This tends to work out to cost, or cost plus pack, plus about 3%. You may be able to do better than these numbers, and it's definitely worth a try. But it's not worth a whole lot of time and anxiety. Cost plus 3%, or cost plus pack (dealer cost) 3%, is okay. If you do that, you've done well.

With vehicles over the $20,000 range, however, things may be a little different. Expensive vehicles can bring you eyeball to eyeball with the problem of scarcity. And scarcity doesn't blink. If demand for the car you want exceeds supply, you are no longer looking at cost plus, you are looking at sticker or sticker plus.

You should still determine dealer cost and negotiate as strongly as possible. But your bargaining power will be greatly reduced by the people coming in behind you who want the same car you do.

A GOOD DEAL ON THE LEASE PAYMENT

When leasing, you have something to consider besides price. Will you want to buy the car eventually or not? Most people don't.

If you will want to buy it, then a good deal payment consists of a combination of things: the lowest payment you can get in conjunction with the lowest buyout that can be coupled to that payment. Normally, reducing one leads to increasing the other: The lower the payment, the higher the buyout. But if you seriously believe you'll buy the car, you want to strike a balance that results in the lowest total amount out of your pocket.

On the other hand, if you don't care about buying, you'll be concerned mainly with the lowest possible monthly payment—which often results in the highest possible buyout. But that will concern you only when it's time to see if you have equity in the car. It's a trade-off: The lower your payment, the less likely you are to have equity at the end of the lease.

Shop lenders for whichever deal is better for you:

- Whether at a car store or lease store, find out who finances their lease deals. Get all of their financing sources, not just the one they use most often. A store of any size will have at least two lenders they habitually use and one to ten others they sometimes use. Ask. If you do not ask, this information will not be offered. The people at the store will try to put your lease through the lender who pays them the most.
- Find out what residual values these lenders use. Some will be higher than others.
- Get payment quotes based on the different programs.
- Do not accept the answer "Let me be honest with you. They're all the same." They are not all the same. Just as different lenders have different home mortgage programs, they also have different auto-leasing programs.
- Be persistent. Don't be embarrassed to repeat yourself. And don't say you "want" to know; say you "have" to know or "need" to know.

I spoke to a salesperson about a $16,300 MSRP car and was quoted $286 per month for 48 months with a $5,000 buyout. I had to ask three times before she told me of a another lender's program offering $273 a month with a buyout of $6,000. If I turned in the car at the end of the lease, the second program would save me $661.

When to Lease

When should you do the deal? Do it in the beginning of the model year. And do it at the end of the month.

The Beginning of the Year

Unless you are certain that the lease rate will go down substantially under a special manufacturer's program, you will have a lower payment if you lease at the beginning of the model year. The car's price will be lower and its residual or lease-end value will be higher. The longer a car has been out, the older it is and the lower its residual value.

For example, in the beginning of the model year the four-year residual-value factor for an Escort will be 32% to 34%. By the end of the year it will have dropped by 4% or 5%. Even without a price increase, this will raise the payment $8 or $9 a month. Over 48 months, that adds up to a nice piece of change.

Not only will the car get older and its residual value go down, but its price will in all probability go up. Manufacturers customarily bump prices at the turn of the calendar year and in the spring. So if you wait for a nice day in June to visit the car stores, you will pay a substantial premium for that good weather.

The End of the Month

For the people in car stores, the end of the month is a time of frenzy. In sales meetings, the managers scream, "Don't let anybody out of here! Write up any offer they make! Get it on paper! We'll take anything! We need business!"

The tirade goes on and on, as the salespeople stare at the walls and ceiling. They hear the same thing almost every month.

Everybody has monthly quotas. The salesperson has a quota, his or her manager has a quota, and the dealership has a quota. Often the quotas are optimistic, so by the end of the month everybody's desperate. And even if the quotas are met, everybody is hungry for that extra deal, that extra buck, to make the month a little better.

SHOULD YOU WAIT TO LEASE A LEFTOVER?

No. In most cases, they're not the bargains they're cracked up to be. Except for cars with limited production runs or cars that are scarce for some other reason, everything is on sale all year long.

Even the exceptions to this are soft exceptions.

Right after the new models are introduced, for example, the managers will use the excitement of newness to try for bigger grosses. For the first few weeks after the new year's cars hit the showroom floor, it will be harder to get a good deal.

But time marches on. When the end of that particular month rolls around, the boys (and girls) will be sitting there staring at their quotas. And pondering their paychecks. No matter how much money they've made, one more deal will make them more. And, lo and behold, it's sale time.

What can you save by waiting till the end of the year? The end of the "year" in car time is August, the month preceding introduction of most of the manufacturer's new line. Unless the model has sold miserably, the price of a car on a lot in August will have risen to the zenith, while its residual will have sunk to its nadir. This combination can raise the 48-month lease payment on a $12,000 to $13,000 car by $20 a month or more. It is highly unlikely that year-end discounts—rarely larger than the Sunday sale discounts—will be large enough to offset so large an increase.

It is also unlikely that the factory's inventory-clearance rebates will offset it. These rebates, to help dealers get rid of their leftovers, run at 3% to 5%. They will be about the same as the factory's price increases during the year. You can see that if the rebates cancel the year's price increases, they merely return you to the original price on a car that still costs considerably more per month because of the lower residual value.

On top of that, these rebates are normally paid to the dealer, not to you. You get a piece of them only if the dealer gives it to you, and he will be generous only if stuck with too many unsold cars. Otherwise, the price will be cost plus pack, plus as much as they can get: just as it was during the year.

Therefore, a month or two after a new car hits the showroom floor, its price should be within two or three hundred of the best deal you can get on a leftover. The higher residual value will compensate for the difference, so you may as well drive the car while it's depreciating and thus benefit from *use value*.

Remember, the day the new models come off the truck, the leftover has a birthday. It is one year older than it was the day before and its value is much less. Lease that leftover and you have lost that value. And gotten nothing in return. Lease the car earlier and, while use will depreciate it a little faster, you will get the value of using and enjoying a new vehicle for the money you are losing.

An old saying in the car business: There's an ass for every seat. Unless the store is choked with inventory, they will wait for the asses to find the seats rather than discount meaningfully (down to cost) at year end.

THE OLD CAR—SELL IT YOURSELF OR TRADE IT IN?

Theoretically, it's better to sell your car yourself. You almost always make more money. Most people are aware of this. And, after discovering what a dealer will pay them in trade, many of them try to sell the car through the newspaper—only to have such a miserable time of it that they come back later and trade it in.

When selling your own car, you need some luck, or you can

spend many hours waiting for people who never show up. And you need to know how to price the car, or you may spend weeks waiting for phone calls that never come.

Determining the Value of Your Used Car

First, I suggest you forget about consumer used-car price guides. Then forget whatever your banker, your insurance agent, or your brother-in-law may have told you. Then forget about the books your banker or insurance agent may have shown you.

Now, find out which used-car price guides are used by the car stores and wholesalers in your area, especially the ones used by wholesalers. Wholesalers buy used cars both at auction and from new-car dealers, then resell them to used-car dealers. They live or die by the prices they put on cars.

The price guides we used were the NADA or National Automobile Dealers Association *Official Used Car Guide*, nicknamed the Yellow Book (available by subscription only, $39 per year, from the Guild Department of NADA, 8400 West Park Drive, McLean, VA, 22102; # (703) 821-7000; also available in some libraries); and the *Black Book*, the real name and a trademark of its publisher, Hearst Business Media Corporation (National Auto Research Division of Hearst Business Media Corporation, PO Box 758, Gainesville, GA, 30503. Subscription $60 per year; # (404) 532-4111). Another wholesale price guide is *The Automotive Market Report*.

The *Black Book*, which comes out every week, was used by Buffalo area wholesalers; in that area, it was the most accurate guide to the cash value of automobiles. But it's no good if it's not used where you live. Find its equivalent at a car store or a lease store and get someone to let you look at it. Read the directions and observe the classifications. Take some care with this. There may be low mileage allowances, and high mileage deductions. There will be big—that is, great big—deductions for diesel engines. There may be additions for certain options. There will be deductions for the lack of certain options. Make sure you deduct for options your car doesn't have.

Then find the value of your car in one of four typical classifications: rough, average, clean, or extra-clean. Try to be accurate about the car's condition. Bear in mind that average is, after all, what most cars actually are.

After the Book, the Real World

Once you have determined the book value of your car, you have to go out into the world and see what reality says. But why bother with the book if you have to go out and face reality anyway? To help keep reality from pulling real wool over your eyes, that's why.

In this case, used-car dealers constitute reality.

Ugh. This may seem like an incredible chore to you, but it's easy. All you have to do is drive around to four or five used-car dealers. A couple of little ones and a couple of big ones. If you want to make things easier with a little white lie, tell them you work for a new car dealer and you are shopping the car for a customer who wants to trade it in. Then say, "Whadda ya gimme for it?" Or whatever a person like you would say.

They may say they don't want the car or they may quote a price. If you get a price, say, "How do you figure that?"

Then, however they justify their price, complain and ask for another two hundred.

See what they say. They might go the deuce, they might go a hun, they might say no and tell you why, they might just shrug and walk away.

Whatever they do, you've got your first offer on the car. Your first price. After you get three or four more and compare them with the book, you will know the wholesale value of your car, its worth in hard dollars, its actual cash value. In short, the price no one will exceed if you trade it in.

But what if you want to sell the car yourself?

To establish your markup, drive around to new-car dealers and find out what they are asking for used cars like yours.

Go to large new-car dealers. Don't visit Smilin' Sam's Used Cars, or Dealin' Dan's Pre-Owned Beauties. You can get wholesale from these guys, but not retail. The new-car dealer's used-car prices will be more predictable and more easily understood. For, generally speaking, his prices will have a closer relation to the quality of the cars. Normally, the dealer will fix up the car, or put on a warranty that will cover most of the cost of surprise repairs, before the car goes over the curb. A new-car dealer will do this because he has more to lose by selling junk than many of the Dealin' Dans of the world.

Be sure to see a reasonably large number of cars. If you look at only two, you may see two that were traded in by the owner's pals. Cars like this will be overpriced in an attempt to recover the money the owner gave away.

Take care not to let your hopes run away with your head when you see the prices on the dealers' cars. Remember, the dealers' easy price for the cars will be $300 or so less than the numbers you see. And he will take off quite a few more hundred for a tough customer. Also, remember the things the dealer will do but you won't: detailing, repairs, inspection, and warranty. If you don't do those things, you probably won't get the money for them, which amounts to a minimum of $150 to $200.

Even though there's an ass for every seat, only a true boob will pay you as much as he will pay a dealer for the same car. So if your buyer starts haggling, and you have to drop your price, keep in mind this difference in value between your car and the dealer's.

But you can indeed put it on before you take it off. The trick is to overprice so you can discount but not to price yourself out of the market. Advertise at about $100 to $150 less than the average dealer price you've found, and you should get phone calls. And that is what you want. You do not want to be stuck with the car for months, paying dollar after dollar to keep it registered and insured—which in some areas can run $30 to $40 a week—as you watch dollar after dollar fall off its value.

If you do sell your own car, try to get your head straight about price. Some people feel, "My car's worth X thousand dollars. If I don't get it, I ain't selling."

These are the people who come back to the dealership and trade in cars worth a few hundred less than they were the first time. Shoot for the moon, but if you want to move the unit, settle for something reasonable.

Questions to Ask Yourself

Are you comfortable with selling things? Many people are not, while others, without even being aware of it, are so blindly enthusiastic that they are terrific natural salespeople.

Do you need a car to drive if the old one sells before you get a new one? Do you have enough space to store the car? Enough time to sell it? If you don't have much time or space, you had better price low and be ready to drop.

If you don't feel comfortable with selling, or you need a new car the moment you let go of the old one, or you have very little time or space, you'll have to forgo the extra money you can make by selling it yourself (but also the potential migraine) and trade it in.

Trading In

Let me remind you that trading in a leased car is, as we say, no-o-o-o problem. It is basically the same as trading an owned car with a lien on it.

If the car is worth more than the lease payoff, that's your equity. Equity is credited against the new lease (deducted from the sell price to lower the acquisition cost), just as if you had traded in a car you owned. If you don't want to use your equity as a downstroke, most dealers will cut you a check.

You can also sell the car yourself. If the lease payoff is, say, $2,000 and you sell it for $2,550, you take the profit.

What You Will Be Paid for Your Trade

You will be paid wholesale or less—the least you'll take. The most you are likely to get is wholesale plus the maximum discount you can negotiate on the new car.

However, you will also effectively receive whatever the sales tax would be on that amount of money. You pay no sales tax on a down payment made with trade equity. On the other hand, in most states cash down is taxed at the standard rate. Put down $2,000 cash in a state that charges 6% and you'll pay another $120 in tax. In effect, then, a trade worth $2,000 will bring you $2120.

Wholesale, or cash value, is called "hard money" or "hard dollars" or simply "hard," as in "two thousand hard." Your discount is known as "show money" or "show dollars."

Most salespeople know these words. But not many know the actual numbers involved. Which doesn't matter anyway, for your salesperson has no say in deciding what your car is worth.

Managers have the say; managers make the decision.

Managers also run the salespeople during deals. They tell them what to say, how much to ask for the store's car, how much to offer for your car, when to offer you more, and so on. They continually ask what you are doing and what you are thinking: trying to figure you out from afar. They question and control the salesperson with varying degrees of strictness, depending on their opinion of his or her ability.

But they control the deal absolutely, deciding how much you will pay for the new car and how much they will pay for your car.

This is an extremely important part of their job. A manager's mandate is to limit as far as possible the amount of money the store invests in trade-ins. Too much money tied up in used cars will kill a car store. This is because almost every deal with a trade represents negative cash flow until the trade is sold.

However, when a deal first appears in the store's bookkeeping, the cash flow is shown as positive. Here's how a manager figures out (washes) a deal with a trade, whether a lease or a buy.

	Selling price		_____
minus	Trade allowance	−	_____
equals	Cash difference	=	_____
plus	Wholesale value of trade	+	_____
equals	Gross	=	_____
minus	Cost of unit (including pack)	−	_____
equals	Net before commission	=	_____

A form like this, called a "wash sheet," is written out for every deal. Every trade taken in is pegged with a wholesale value. So the manager's evaluation of your car appears instantly and stays there forever, for everyone to see. You can imagine how much the manager wants to be right.

Although the wholesale value of the trade is entered on the wash sheet as a positive number, that money does not, in fact, exist until your car is sold. And the salesperson's commission, if paid before someone buys your car, also represents negative cash flow: money paid out before it comes in.

To illustrate, suppose you were trading in a car worth $2,100 hard on a new car listed at $10,000 and marked up $1,000 after the pack. You come in wanting $3,100 for your car. Obviously, you won't get it, for that would be $1,000 over its cash value: an even swap with a bottom line of zero. After a long negotiation, you finally accept $2,725. That's your trade allowance, "show dollars." The salesman "shows you $2,725."

Here's how the manager would wash the deal.

	Selling price		$10,000
minus	Allowance	−	2,725
equals	Cash difference	=	$ 7,275
plus	Wholesale value of trade	+	2,100
equals	Gross	=	$ 9,375
minus	Cost of unit	−	9,000
equals	Net before commission	=	$ 375

The "net before commission" you see here is also called the "gross profit," or simply "the gross." This is a small one. Big grosses are, of course, everybody's dream but yours.

Notice that although a profit is shown, what you are actually leasing the car for is $7,275, the cash difference. When the store drafts on the lease contract (requests and receives payment), that's what the lessor will pay. The store, however, will have to pay the factory or the bank that financed the car approximately $8,500: the $9,000 minus the pack and the holdback. The store will be in the red for about $1,225. And if the salesperson receives a commission of $100 or so before your car is sold, the store will be in the red for $1,325.

I'm going through this so you understand what "wholesale value" and "actual cash value" really mean and how great the pressure is not to exceed them. They refer to the amount of money your car can be sold for immediately, the very next day if necessary, to turn the deal into positive cash flow: sold either at the auction or to the used-car dealer down the block. Very few stores can afford to have a bunch of money-losing deals sitting around without knowing precisely when they can be turned into money-making deals.

But, you may ask, since wholesale value is an estimate, how can it be considered "hard" money? Because the selling prices of used cars are monitored daily and the results published every week. That's why I emphasized finding the right used-car price guide. The books wholesalers use report the amounts various cars brought at auction sales no longer ago than the previous week. Subtract a few dollars and that's what your car will bring this week.

What does this mean to you?

1. No matter where you do the deal, no matter how you try to negotiate—whether you start by hiding the fact that you have a trade, or start by emphasizing what you want for the trade, or start with everything at once—you will not be paid more than actual cash value. But if you don't find out what that is ahead of

time, you may be paid less and still receive what seems to be a magnificent sum as a trade allowance.

2. If you want to know the price you're paying to lease your new car, you must know the cash value of your trade. You can't work from discount or trade allowance. The price of your car will equal the cash difference plus the cash value of the trade. Add the two and that's the price. Subtract the cost of the unit with pack and that's the dealer's profit.

WHERE TO DO THE DEAL

Picking the place to lease a car isn't easy. Not only is a lease deal more complicated than a buy, but since lease stores are definitely worth checking out, there are simply more places to call or visit.

Let's start with dealerships.

Unlike lease stores, dealers are married to a manufacturer. In other words, you'll get your first price from a place that theoretically stands behind and services its product, and whose policy, or official policy, is to keep you happy in order to earn your repeat business and to retain the manufacturer's franchise.

Begin with a conveniently located, big dealer that has a reputation for dealing: one that advertises itself as a high-volume, low-profit store. If, however, you live in an area where the stores are few and far between and the dealers feel like they're giving away their cabin cruisers when they knock a hundred dollars off a price, call a lease store first. Get the lease store's price and payment quote before visiting the dealership.

Why start with the big guy, who has to pay all that overhead?

First, at a big dealership, you'll be able to see and handle more cars. This may make it easier to make the final decision on color, options, and so on.

Second, you need some kind of starting price to serve as a benchmark or basis for comparison. With most big dealers, as with most retail stores, size means volume and volume means discounts. Or, at least, the possibility of discounts.

Third, and probably most important, size indicates a desire to grow.

To grow, a store has to get more cars from the manufacturer. And it cannot get them simply by asking. You can't call Detroit and say, "Hey, send me fifteen extra Mustangs next month, will ya?"

To get more cars, the store has to sell its allotment or more than its allotment. It has to sell everything it is currently getting before the factory will ship it more. A dealer who wants to grow will usually sell for a small profit simply to move the unit—so he can get more units to move.

Next, obviously, the store should have a reputation for honesty and good service.

Check with the Better Business Bureau. Ask friends, relatives, acquaintances, people you work with. The problem here is that one man's good deal is the next man's ripoff; one man's day at the beach with a service department is the next man's nightmare. Bear in mind that the nicest bunch of people in the most honest store on earth will not resist the temptation to rip off a customer when the opportunity presents itself.

If you happen to know someone at a local dealership, ask them what the place is like. Interpret their answer in terms of what you know about them. If the person you know is not a salesperson, ask about the other stores around town. They may have heard something, good or bad, that will help you decide.

Generally, it's probably better to know and ask someone other than a salesperson. For, despite you being okay, and me being okay, and almost everybody being okay, you can't expect most people to tell you the truth if the truth will set them back an appreciable sum of money.

Next, this big, high-volume dealer who enjoys a good reputation and is conveniently located should sell the manufacturer's lease program. I think it's a good idea to use the price and payment derived from the manufacturer's lease program for your benchmark, your first point of comparison.

This is not to say you won't be able to beat that deal. Quite possibly, you will. However, the factory credit companies are big, rich institutions: They are actually more stable than many banks and their pricing and policies will be relatively stable. With Ford Credit, Chrysler Credit, GMAC, or Toyota Credit, you know, more or less, what you are dealing with.

You are dealing with subsidiaries of the manufacturers.

As such, they have goals that banks do not. Like banks, they exist to make a profit from the money they lend. But they also exist to help move the manufacturer's cars. If they fail to do so, their managers will be looking for new jobs.

Thus, they have to be a little sensitive to your feelings about your deal. If you have bad feelings about the deal, you may well have bad feelings about your car, a car built by their employer. Banks and lease stores may not care if you become alienated from the factory's products because you were fooled by a lease contract. But Ford and General Motors care quite a bit; therefore, so do Ford Credit and GMAC.

They're not going to feed your cat and water your plants for you, of course, but here's an example. Once, I hammered a guy on a truck lease. Got him for five hundred over sticker. Sold, signed, and delivered. However, a month after he took the truck, Ford Credit mailed him a new contract. It charged him a lower payment, essentially leasing him the truck at sticker price. Ford Credit didn't want him getting angry at Ford if somebody happened to tell him how much he was paying.

A bank wouldn't have bothered.

What to Look for at a Dealership

Look for the signs that indicate good management: cleanliness and orderliness, cheerful and friendly personnel, up-to-date, well-maintained facility and equipment, and so on.

Check the hours that the service department is open. Longer

hours means more convenience for you. And longer hours also means more mechanics and thus a better chance for prompt service.

Wander around, if you can, in the service department. Hang out by the Parts Department window. See if people are kidding around or snarling at each other. See if the mechanics are complaining about unavailable parts.

After you lease your car, the most important thing about the dealership will be how fast and how well the service department can fix it if it breaks. But the mechanics can't fix the car unless Parts supplies the part. And at our store, all too often we did not have, and had to wait a long time for, the part a customer needed.

The reason was simple. The owner was unwilling to spend the money (lots of it) needed to maintain a parts inventory large enough to match our volume of business.

Our whole Service Department suffered from insufficient funds. Just as we had too few parts, we also had too few mechanics for the volume of business we did.

This is probably the most common source of dealership service problems. But it's hard to discover. If you know someone in the car business, ask about it. If you don't, try asking the Parts guys about the size of their inventory. The bigger it is, the more money invested in it, the better for you.

FLASHING RED WARNING LIGHTS: DEALER ADDENDA

Dealer addenda or dealer add-ons are things the dealer adds to the car, whether you want them or not, then charges you for.

Probably the most common of the add-ons is a "protection package" composed of rustproofing, paint shield, fabric guard, and, sometimes, sound deadening. The next most common is striping, sometimes lots of striping and a few other things which all add up to a "decor group." Retail price on protection packages and decor groups represents a markup of 200% to 300% over their cost.

Suppose you are leasing or for some other reason want no part of a protection package. But the car you want at the dealer most convenient for you has a sticker on the window saying the stuff is already installed.

Look in the wheel wells and under the hood to see if the metal body parts wear a thin coating of yellowish goop. This is the rustproofing, and there's a chance it won't be there. The window sticker may be a bluff, designed to fake you into thinking you have to pay for all this stuff and give the dealer an extra $400 or so profit on the car.

Why might it be a bluff? Because in a competitive market, no dealer likes to spend nickel one on a car before someone has committed to buy it.

But if the rustproofing has been sprayed on the car and if the salesperson tells you that you can't get one of their cars without the protection package, leave. That protection package, which should be called a "profit package," will cost the dealer $150 to $200, mostly for the insurance policy behind the rustproofing warranty. The price to you, however, will probably be $600 to $750.

Don't mess around, don't dicker, don't listen to the salesperson if she tells you she will take the price of the package off the price of the car. She's giving you a phony discount of $600 or so (a real discount of around $200) to club you with when you ask for big dollars off the price of the car. Walk out and go somewhere else.

Loaner Availability

If you lease a car from a dealership, your right to and your chance of getting a service loaner (a car to drive while yours is being repaired) are exactly the same as if you buy.

Loaner availability, however, is not often a good way to choose between dealerships. For when you ask about them, no

salesperson in their right mind will tell you that you cannot
have one.

Even a big dealer cannot possibly afford to keep enough
loaners around for every new-car customer who wants one. And
used-car customers want loaners, too. So what happens is that if
your problem can be scheduled for service a week or two in
advance, you can usually get a loaner.

But if you need service right away, there's a good chance all
the loaners will be out. But you will not necessarily be stuck. If
someone will intercede for you (usually a salesperson hoping for
repeat business or a recommendation), many dealers will put
you out in a used car with dealer plates while yours is being
fixed.

LEASE STORES

After you've found a dealership or two with a reasonably good
reputation for honesty and quality of service, you have another
alternative to consider.

Lease stores take your description of car and options, then
come up with a price and a payment. If you accept the deal and
order the car, the lease store gets it from a car store, delivers it to
you, collects your front money and presents you with a lease
contract to sign. Afterward, like dealerships, most will assign the
lease to a bank, which pays the lease store, sends you a coupon
book, and collects your payments. A few lease stores finance the
deals themselves, sometimes by borrowing from a bank, then
making payments to the bank out of the payments you make to
them.

The advantages lease stores claim in their ads are these:

1. Wider selection.
2. No high-pressure sales tactics.
3. Lower price.

An advantage they don't advertise is this. Unlike dealerships, many lease stores will quote prices over the phone. The reputable ones give you accurate quotes, for lease stores sell prices, not cars. This makes it easier to compare one against another, and also to construct for yourself a range, an array of prices and payments, which makes it easier to compare everybody against everybody else.

Let me poke a few holes in the advertised advantages so you know what to be skeptical about.

1. *Wider selection* Lease stores are not franchisees of any particular manufacturer. They will lease you any brand of car that they can obtain from a dealership. But so will many dealerships. The Buffalo Ford store would lease you a Cadillac or a Mercedes, if you wanted one. But we didn't advertise the fact. The problem with the wider selection at the lease store is that you can't see or handle the merchandise at the same place you do the deal. You have to go to two places.

2. *No high-pressure sales tactics* Most lease stores employ salespeople who work on commission. If you don't encounter some form of pressure, you have stumbled across a salesperson who has lost the will to live.

3. *Lower price* Maybe, maybe not. When you call a lease store, some will tell you that they can beat a dealer's price because they buy cheap owing to the manufacturer's fleet incentive program. The salesperson will say he can lease you a car for a lower price than any dealer will offer.

He may be right. But that doesn't make the rest of what he says necessarily and completely true.

First, as mentioned, fleet incentives vary. Try to find out how much the discount actually is. If it is more than $100 or so, find out, or figure out, how much of it is being taken off your price.

Second, payments vary, too. Check the lease store's payment carefully. The bank financing the deal may charge more or less than the factory credit company; or more or less than the bank financing a local car store's leases. Compare them carefully. At this point you should be able to begin the comparison, since you've gotten from a dealership a payment quote based on factory financing.

Then, as with a dealership, find out how many lenders the lease store has access to and who they are. If there are more than one, compare payments from each. Payments can vary as much as $10 a month from bank to bank.

If the store finances its own deals, it may be a sign that the place has been successful long enough to amass substantial capital. Which may mean that it will be around for a while longer: a definite plus. But check the store's track record; don't take it on faith.

A self-financing lease store, however, may not be doing the volume of business necessary to give you the best available rate. So check its payments against those of banks. If the self-financed store's payment is higher, you have to balance the benefit of doing business with a company that has been in business long enough to establish contacts throughout the automotive community (if you discover such to be the case) against the drawback of a higher payment.

How much is this benefit worth? That's up to you. Here's a brief scenario from which it is missing.

You get a great payment from a little store. The salesman says—and you confirm—that an agreement exists with a dealership to provide repair work under the warranty.

The little store goes out of business. Your car breaks. You call the service department at the dealership. The service writer tells you they are no longer doing warranty work for the little, defunct lease store's customers. Now what?

Besides the fact that's it's sensible to shop, the other reason to check lease store prices and payments carefully is that lease stores function, as businesses, like car stores. Their profit comes from marking up the merchandise, marking up their service, and marking up the interest rate on the loan. (Your payment's lease or interest charges will include a commission to the store.)

If the store can find a way to hide some of that markup, it will.

And it can find a way. It can find a number of ways, for the laws governing lease loans are a good deal less stringent than those governing installment purchase loans. As we shall see, even stores owned by reputable institutions may employ complicated tricks to hide the true markup. So a deal may not be as good as it seems, even though the quoted price sounds unbeatable.

Like car stores, lease stores don't "give" you a good deal. You have to get one.

Disadvantages

- Many lease stores have no service departments.
- Many do not accept trade-ins.
- At some stores, the people may not know anything about cars. And a car is what you'll be driving, not a method of financing. At other lease stores, however, there will be people who know a whole lot about cars.
- If the store doesn't hold its own paper, it has no need for you when the deal is done.
- Lease stores have no brand-name loyalty, and are not disciplined by a manufacturer.
- Some lease stores are started on a fast shuffle and a muttered prayer. Your store may go out of business a few months after you do your deal.

All of this can add up to a lot of inconvenience. And a great big headache if you need repair work done under the manufacturer's warranty. Then you'll have to go to a dealer who may treat you as if you were a three-headed bug.

Some dealerships will do warranty work on cars bought elsewhere; others will not. And if the schedule is crowded, any dealer will assign your problems a lower priority than a customer's. You may not like this, but if you were in the dealer's shoes, you would do the same thing.

So when considering a lease store:

- See if it can handle your trade, if you have one.
- Find out how long it has been in business—and try to make an estimate of the probability it will stay in business. You may not be an investment banker, but go with your gut feeling.
- Ask if the store has a service arrangement with a repair shop or a dealership. If the answer is yes, call the shop or dealership. Make sure the arrangement exists, make sure it will last the entire length of your warranty and/or lease term, and make sure you are not paying extra for it.

Do the Advantages of a Lease Store Outweigh the Disadvantages?

If you want a car not handled by any of the local car stores, yes—obviously, you have no choice.

If you are in an area where the car stores are few and far between—and therefore try to eliminate discounts—quite possibly. A smart lease store working with a smart bank may offer payments that blow the local dealers out of the water.

Character may give you an answer. A half mile away from your house, the most honest and helpful guy in town may be running a lease store that's been in business for 20 years.

If the place you're considering checks out, all that's left to consider is the economics of the deal. Here's a checklist to help you compare deals.

THE ECONOMICS OF THE DEAL

☐ Closed- or open-end lease _____

☐ Amount of security deposit
(less is more—for you, that is) _____

☐ MSRP _____

☐ Factory discounts _____

☐ Sticker price _____

- [ ] Store discount _____
- [ ] Sell price _____
- [ ] Lease or interest rate _____
- [ ] Residual-value factor (percentage of MSRP) _____
- [ ] Residual value amount _____
- [ ] Payment _____
- [ ] Lease-end purchase option? _____
- [ ] Any charge for purchase option? _____
- [ ] Lease-end buyout amount _____
- [ ] Total cost if you don't buy at lease end _____
- [ ] Total cost if you do buy at lease end _____
- [ ] Option to buy during term? _____
- [ ] Prepayment penalties? How much? _____
- [ ] What happens in case of total loss? _____
- [ ] Gap insurance available? _____
- [ ] Condition of car at end of term: any zingers? _____
- [ ] Liability and collision insurance requirement _____
- [ ] Number of miles included in payment _____
- [ ] Excess-mileage penalty (if applicable) _____
- [ ] Trade allowance (if applicable) _____
- [ ] Cash value offered for your trade (if applicable) _____
- [ ] Disposition Fee? _____ How much? _____

With this information, you should be able to make a pretty full comparison between different cars and different deals.

NOTE: If you want the performance model of a standard nameplate, you may have to look harder for a good deal. Many lenders, assuming that performance cars will be abused, lower their residuals 3% to 5% below the standard models. This raises the lease payment significantly.

In the used-car market, however, these relatively rare vehicles are much more expensive than standard models with comparable amenities. Even at wholesale, they bring a thousand dollars more. Some lenders take this into account, but you may have to search to find them. As before, if low payment is your primary concern, shop for the highest residual. If convinced you'll buy the vehicle and have some flexibility on the payment, shop for the deal with the least overall cost.

THE RELATIONSHIP BETWEEN PRICE AND PAYMENT

Whatever kind of car you want, be sure to double-check the relationship between the sell price and the payment. As we shall see, one place may charge you a higher sell price than another, charge you a higher lease rate, use the same residual value, and yet charge you the same, or even less, per month—which adds up to charging you the same, or less, period.

This can happen because different lenders use different methods of calculating or, more accurately, inflating lease payments. Since payments can be inflated, the relationship between price and payment is not necessarily constant. Do not, therefore, follow the advice on leasing sometimes given by very bright people: to concentrate only on the vehicle's price. Simply put, that's wrong. It can cost you.

You do need to pay attention to price. You do need to force the salesperson to quote price accurately. Then you need to do what the salesperson or manager does: move fluidly among cost, price, cash difference (if there's a trade), and payment. If you lose sight of any of the elements in the deal, you are likely to be fooled. Not because anyone is going to do anything special in your case, but just as a matter of routine. As we shall see in Chapter Four (page 110), some salespeople will quote payments so far beyond what you need to pay that it's almost obscene. They wouldn't do this if it didn't work.

How to Calculate Lease Payments

To avoid being fooled and thus to save money when you lease a car, you must be able to calculate payments. Trying to find out what's going on by acting suspicious, playing the role of the "tough customer," and trying to force your salesperson and/or manager to explain everything will not necessarily result in either the truth or a good deal.

One of my customers tried to do just that. Instead of an explanation, he got a flimflam in spades.

This was the guy I hammered on the truck lease. He had factory-ordered a Ranger, Ford's little pickup. One fine Saturday it arrived at the store. I called him up and, about ten minutes before closing time, he came in to look at it.

It had been a very slow Saturday. The owner's son-in-law and I were the only people left in the store.

My customer was happy with the truck, but was no longer happy with the deal. While waiting, he had figured out, or thought he figured out, that he hadn't received enough of a discount on the vehicle. We, of course, were convinced that he had received more than enough.

We went to work on him. We pulled out the contract and the original purchase order. We flashed the lease charts at him, saying here's the factor for this, here's the factor for that.

Then we showed him the buy chart and said, here's the factor for 9.5% (the lease rate he was being charged) and told him how to figure the principal on a loan. And, after dividing the factor into his payment, we came up with a principal of $7,000.

That, we told him, was what he was paying for the truck. Seven thousand dollars. (Sticker was about ninety-two hundred.) Was that a super discount, or what?

He had to admit it. It was one hell of a discount. It was damn near the deal of the century. He took the deal, took the truck and went away happy.

As I mentioned, a month later Ford Credit sent him a new

contract charging him a lower payment. The payment I had talked him into, and we had successfully defended for more than an hour of very suspicious questioning, was five hundred over sticker.

And this guy was not dumb. Not at all. Intuitively, he had achieved an insight into something most customers never catch a glimmer of. But, like the boss said, there was no way for him to figure it out. He couldn't back up his insight with numbers.

Here, then, are the numbers: some of the methods of calculating lease payments. One is the way we did it on the deals we put through Ford Credit. Another is the no-frills, basic method, also called the Depreciation Method. Since most lenders add frills to squeeze extra money from the basic method, the third is from the gigantic bank that financed our 60-month leases. This Bank Method is like the basic one, but makes it obvious where the extra juice comes from: the addition of a $200 bank fee. Finally, there are a few words about financial calculators and the method behind them. In the Appendix, you will find examples of charts containing residual value factors.

Although there are other methods of calculation, these are highly typical. If you use them to calculate a payment on a Hyundai or a Porsche, you should be very close. If you are not close, you should take the trouble to find out why. Later, when we go shopping for prices, you will learn *how* to find out why.

Two things you should understand going in:

1. Most lease payments—even when you get a good deal— have a little extra juice built in. For example, using a financial calculator to figure out the payment on our sample Escort ($8,000 sell price, $2,920 residual, 9.5% lease rate, 48-month term) will yield a monthly payment of $149.56. Ford calls the extra money contained in a payment calculated with its factors an administrative fee. Other lenders may use different terminology. One way to hold a consistent concept from lender to lender is to regard the extra money as coming from either a higher sell price or a lower residual value.

Thus, if you raise the Escort's sell price by $321, the calculator will show a payment of $157.56, our old friend from Chapter Two. Or if you retain the $8,000 sell price and use a residual of $2,451.31, the calculator will again give you $157.56.

Does this residual value, a figure between $2,400 and $2,500, ring any bells for you? It was what we said you would be likely to get for your four-plus-year-old average Escort if you sold it yourself. In other words, it's a price that's not too hard to get. Lenders who set up good deals by using hard-to-get prices as lease buyouts are lenders who set themselves up for trouble.

2. Lease rates and residual values change. Lease rates may go up, down, and up again by the time you read this. What you have here are tools with which to learn and compare, not gospel.

How We Did It at the East Babbit Ford Store

Here's how we figured payments on the leases we wrote through Ford Motor Credit.

Residual Value and Residual Value Factor The residual value factor is the percentage of MSRP used to calculate the dollar amount of a car's residual or lease-end value after the amount of time the lease will run. To find it, call a Ford dealer, a dealership selling the brand you want, a lease store, or a bank. They'll tell you: residuals are not kept secret.

Multiply MSRP before package discounts by the factor. For example, 32% (.32) as in the case of our Escort. The car's MSRP was $9,126. .32 × $9,126 = $2,920.32. The Escort's residual or lease-end value is $2,920.32.

For our $16,500 T-Bird with the $17,000 MSRP, Ford's 48-month residual value factor is 34%. .34 × $17,000 = $5,780. The Bird's residual value after four years is $5,780.

(These factors are from January charts. Residual values drop as time goes by. New charts are issued every two months.

Residuals will be highest when the model is introduced, usually September or October.)

Residual Value Credit Factor Now we would consult a chart. What you would do is call or visit a Ford dealer and play footsy with a salesperson or the Leasing Manager. They will have a chart with two columns of factors. One will contain the acquisition cost (or capitalized cost) payment factors. The other, our concern for the moment, will hold the residual value or lease-end value credit (or deduction) factors.

Footsy is an implied promise of future business. Talk the salesperson into telling you what the factors are for the current interest rate and length of lease term you want. (Get factors for longer and shorter terms and higher and lower rates, too. And if the salesperson is helpful, what the heck, you may as well deliver on your implied promise.) Write down the factors.

Now, the residual value credit factor is used to determine how much will be deducted from the acquisition cost payment to compensate for the car's value at the end of the lease.

To get that amount, multiply the residual value by the residual, or lease-end, value credit factor. For a 48-month lease with a rate of 9.5%, Ford's factor is .017071. On the Escort, then, the residual value of $2,920.32 is multiplied by .017071. .017071 × $2,920.32 = $49.85. This residual value credit will be subtracted from the acquisition cost payment to arrive at the lease payment.

Acquisition Cost, Acquisition Cost Payment Factor, and Acquisition Cost Payment NOTE: Some lenders use the term "capitalized cost" or "cap cost" to mean the same thing as "acquisition cost." Both terms refer to the capital the lender/lessor puts out to acquire the car and that you partially pay off (plus interest, of course) to acquire the lease on the car.

Acquisition cost (or cap cost) is calculated as follows:

	MSRP
minus	Package discounts (if any)
equals	Sticker price
minus	Store discount
equals	Sell price
minus	Cash down (if any, from you or from a factory rebate)
and minus	Trade equity put down (if any)
plus	Balance owed on trade (if any)
plus	Cost of dealer add-ons or any extras you purchase
equals	Acquisition cost

The Escort began with an MSRP of $9,126. Package discount took us down to $8,419. We negotiated a store discount of $419, leaving a sell price of $8,000. We put nothing down, we traded nothing in, we owed nothing, we bought nothing extra, so the sell price of $8,000 was our acquisition cost.

To get the acquisition cost factor, we have asked at the dealership (or looked it up, if we have the charts). For 48 months at a lease rate of 9.5%, Ford's factor is .025926. Multiply the acquisition or capitalized cost by this factor to derive the aquisition cost payment. $8,000 × .025926 = $207.41, our acquisition cost payment.

Monthly Lease Payment To get the monthly payment, we subtract the residual value credit from the acquisition cost payment. $207.41 − $49.85 = $157.56, the lease payment based on our $8,000 deal price. It excludes taxes.

Summary:

1. The MSRP before factory discounts multiplied by the residual value factor equals the residual value.
2. The discounted price, minus any cash or trade equity put down (plus balance owed on the trade, if any) equals the acquisition or capitalized cost.

3. Acquisition or capitalized cost multiplied by the acquisition cost payment factor from the chart or salesperson equals the acquisition cost payment.
4. The residual value amount multiplied by the residual value *credit* factor equals the residual value deduction from the acquisition payment.
5. Acquisition payment minus this deduction equals the lease payment.

THE BASIC OR DEPRECIATION METHOD

Many lenders look for a little extra money: a little here, a little there, a little somewhere else. But here's the method most of them start with.

The lease payment is divided into two parts.

1. You pay off the estimated amount that the car will depreciate during the lease (or amortize the depreciation).
2. You pay interest, sometimes called lease charges. That interest, computed with the money factor or lease factor, is charged on the *total* money (acquisition cost plus residual value) that the lender considers to be at risk.

The acquisition cost (sometimes called capitalized cost) is derived as just shown. And so is the residual value. But each lender decides for itself what percentage will be used as the residual value factor and each lender prints up its own charts. You have to call around to find out what factors your lenders are using, just as you must call to find out what their lease rates are. Then:

1. Acquisition cost minus residual value amount equals depreciation.
2. Depreciation divided by the number of months in the lease equals the monthly depreciation payment.

3. Acquisition cost plus residual value equals total money.
4. Total money multiplied by the money or lease factor equals the monthly interest payment or monthly lease charge.
5. Monthly depreciation plus monthly interest payment equals your monthly lease payment. Plus tax.

Here's how to calculate the payment on the Escort lease using Ford's residual value and interest rate.

Sell price	$ 8,000.00	(acquisition cost, since there's no downstroke and no balance to be paid off)
Residual value	− 2,920.00	
48 months' depreciation	$ 5,080.00	
Monthly depreciation	$ 105.83	($5,080 ÷ 48)
Sell price	$ 8,000.00	
Residual value	+ 2,920.00	
Total money	$10,920.00	
Money factor	× .00396	(for 9.5% lease rate)
Interest or lease charge	$ 43.24	
Monthly lease payment	$ 149.07	(monthly depreciation + interest)

The payment is $8.49 lower than Ford's. We saw that Ford factors are built on a residual lower than the one stated. You cannot, however, say to your Ford salesman, "You're wrong," because Ford can use whatever residual it wants when figuring out its factors.

What you can say—after you figure out the actual residual—is "I want my guaranteed buyout to be the same as the residual used to calculate the payment."

The Bank Method

Like many banks, the one that financed our 60-month paper added a bank fee to the acquisition cost, effectively raising the sell price of the car. The one we used charged $200. Some banks charge more, some less; some charge no fee, and some charge no stated fee but have hidden charges built into their calculations.

Our bank's lease rate of 10.8% and money factor of .0045 appear high. Notice in the following example, however, that while the rate is not competitive, the payment is—because the residual value is high and because the stated residual is actually used to calculate the payment.

Here's how the Escort calculations would have looked if put through the bank, which called the acquisition cost plus bank fee the "Net Agreed Value":

Sell price	$ 8,000.00	
Bank acquisition fee	+ 200.00	
Net agreed value (acquisition cost + bank fee)	$ 8,200.00	
Residual value	− 3,376.00	(37% of MSRP of $9,126)
48 months' depreciation	$ 4,824.00	
Monthly depreciation payment	$ 100.50	($4,824 ÷ 48)
Sell price	$ 8,000.00	
Residual value	+ 3,376.00	
Total money	$11,576.00	
Money factor	× .0045	(for 10.8% lease rate)
Interest or lease charge	$ 52.09	
Monthly lease payment	$ 152.59	(monthly depreciation + interest)

As you can see, the payment is highly competitive. Why? The residual value is not merely high, it is from Lala Land. And that's what to look for when shopping for a good lease deal: a residual from Lala Land. If you find one, however, be careful to check:

- That it is actually used to calculate the payment
- That it's a percentage of MSRP, not the sell price—i.e., that both the factor (percentage) and the dollar amount are high, for a formula could be worked out using a high percentage of a low amount, resulting in a low residual and a high payment
- And that the contract does not require you to return a car in clean retail condition. You want it to require average condition. Average is not clean. The difference starts at about $500 and rises swiftly. And if the lease requires a clean car and yours is average, that difference comes from you.

How to Derive the Money Factor

In our examples we've seen money factors of .0045 and .00396. You derive the money factor by dividing the quoted interest rate or lease rate by 24. Thus 10.8% = .108 ÷ 24 = .0045; and 9.5% = .095 ÷ 24 = .0039583. Rounded up in the lender's favor, this equals .00396—or, quite possibly, .004.

If you know the money factor and want the lease or interest rate, you perform the reverse operation. .00396 × 24 = .09504, or 9.5%, rounded off. And .0045 × 24 = .108, or 10.8%.

Financial Calculators (Interest in Advance Method)

If you have a financial calculator, you probably use it to calculate the payments on "regular" loans (fully amortized, with balances that decline to zero and interest calculated on the declining balance).

It will probably calculate lease payments, too, if you change the keystrokes slightly.

The calculators I'm familiar with compute a lease payment as if it were a loan for the acquisition cost, with a payout based on the amount of the depreciation, and a balloon payment (one huge payment) at the end of the loan for the amount of the residual value. The monthly interest on this loan is paid in advance, at the beginning of the month, before you have had use of the money for that month. The monthly interest on a "regular" loan is paid in arrears, or after you've had the money for a month.

Therefore, when calculating a lease payment, you change the keystrokes to tell the machine to figure the interest in the beginning of the month rather than the end. And since the future value of a lease loan (or balance at the end of the term) is not zero, but the residual value amount, you key in the residual and convert it to a negative amount. Check your direction booklet. With a 48-month lease, this method normally calculates a payment about $.50 to $1.00 a month higher than the depreciation method, depending on the cost of the car.

You don't have a financial calculator? Don't worry about it. They can be fun, but you don't need one.

Work through the very simple arithmetic laid out above. Practice with different prices and residuals. Do it! Learning is like love. The first jolt comes easy, but afterward, if you won't work for it, it won't work for you.

And don't worry if it isn't second nature to you. Although the arithmetic is easy, the concepts may be new and may take a little getting used to.

Then, before going out to shop for price, calculate lease payments on a whole range of prices, from 10% over sticker all the way down to cost and below. We'll talk more about this in the chapter on doing the deal.

When doing the deal, if the payments quoted seem somehow "off," have the salesperson go through the calculations with you. Check and verify each factor and each step. If the salesperson doesn't know how to calculate payments (a surprisingly large number don't) and the manager is doing it for him or her, have the salesperson get the manager to demonstrate the calculations.

A slip of the finger on a calculator button could cost you a nice piece of change.

If your salesperson is unwilling to do this, then that person is not willing to work hard enough to earn your business. Tell them so, in exactly those words. They have been taught, repeatedly, that it takes hard work to earn a customer's business, so saying that should push a button.

And now that we know a little about what we're doing, let's talk briefly about advertisements, then put our knowledge into action and do some shopping.

READING THE ADS

Many people start to shop by sitting down. Then they read the ads in the newspaper.

PAINLESS PAYMENTS!   LEASE IT OR LOSE IT!
LUXURY FOR LESS!   SAVE! SAVE! SAVE!!!

What do car ads tell you? Not much. The most useful information appearing in car ads in the newspapers is news about factory cash rebates and factory-subsidized low interest rates. But there are a few tendencies the ads may indicate.

1. You can get an idea of the relative prices of cars.

For example, the Sunday automotive section advertised a Pontiac Grand Am LE Coupe with a standard transmission for $10,500. A bit farther on, I saw a Pontiac Grand Prix with a little less equipment but an automatic transmission. The price was $12,200, about $40 a month more on a GMAC 48-month lease.

Now, this may have been a bait-and-switch price. But it would provide a rough notion of how much more I would have to spend to lease the larger and, to my way of thinking, nicer car.

2. You can get an idea of which dealers are dealing low.

The $10,500 Grand Am above was a stick. A few pages

farther on, I found an automatic Grand Am with a tad more equipment for $10,645. With the extra options and the automatic transmission, this car is worth $700 more than the other. If I wanted a Grand Am, I'd go first to the store that featured seven hundred dollars more car for one hundred forty-five more dollars.

3. You may be able to get an idea of the relative cost of lease payments for different vehicles.

For example, an ad touted a Pontiac Sunbird for a price of $10,000 and a 60-month lease payment of $179. The Grand Am, although $10,500, was also $179 a month for 60 months. Reason? The Grand Am's residual value is 4% higher than the Sunbird's.

Farther along was an Acura Integra, more expensive than either Pontiac but with a 60-month lease payment lower than both at $169. The Integra's residual is 6% to 8% higher than the Grand Am's. If you had started out thinking Sunbird, then read those ads, you may have ended up thinking Integra.

The Rest of the Stuff in the Ads: Common Come-ons

The basic technique of car ads is the bait and switch. Something wonderful provokes your excitement and desire—but turns out to be unavailable. Your excitement is then refocused, and your desire switched to something else. Here are a few of its common forms.

Price and Payment for One Car Only You see a terrific lease payment in great big print. But when you read the tiny print you find a stock or VIN number (*vehicle identification number,* i.e., serial number). When the store identifies the advertised vehicle with a number, that particular vehicle is the only one the store is legally obligated to sell at the advertised price.

That vehicle may be the most unpopular color of the decade. Or it may be exactly what you want. If it is what you want, there's a good chance that it already will have been sold.

Price and Payment Excluding Freight Charges This little number was the favorite of the store that was five minutes down the road: the store that came in either right behind us or right ahead of us in Ford's monthly sales figures.

Of course, the ad does tell you that freight is excluded from the ad price. In the tiny print.

Payment Calculated with Cash Down This was our favorite. We advertised fabulous payments in big, bold graphics. Down at the bottom, the small print would say that the payment was based on a down payment of thousands of dollars in cash or trade equity.

Excited customers would walk in waving the newspaper and ask eagerly to see the car. The moment always came, however, when the salesperson would have to acquaint the customer with the facts. Then you'd hear the customer start to yell. Then you'd see the customer walk out.

These gimmicks are more common than houseflies. Don't be fooled.

The Mystery Vehicle with the Magic Residual This gimmick promotes a bank lease program or a factory lease program, rather than a particular car. The ad will mention an unnamed vehicle at some price and with some residual value. If you take the trouble to discover what percentage of price the residual represents, you will find the percentage to be extremely high. So high, in fact, that perhaps only 3% of the cars in existence retain their value that well. You thus have three chances in a hundred that the car you want will have a payment similar to the one in the ad.

Do not count on advertised sale prices to save you money. Look for the kick in the head in the tiny print. If it isn't there, be prepared for it when you go to the store. Remember, as long as supply exceeds demand, you can lease a car yesterday or tomorrow for the price that is advertised as today's only. If you know how.

FOUR

Putting It Together: Shopping

Let's assume now that we are going to lease a Ford Taurus GL for four years. The car has a three-liter V-6 engine, an automatic overdrive transmission, and Equipment Package 204A, which includes air conditioner, cruise control, tilt steering wheel, power mirrors, power windows, power locks, power driver's seat, rear window defogger, interval wipers, light group, digital clock, a decorative pinstripe, and finned wheel covers. Options on the car as priced but not included in the package are: white-wall tires, clearcoat paint, and a stereo radio with cassette player. Power steering and brakes are standard.

The MSRP is $15,826. A $500 package discount brings the sticker price down to $15,326.

Assume also that we have bought a cost and price guide and have determined cost on the car as follows:

	Cost
Base	$10,231
Freight	+ 426
Engine and Transmission	+ 571

Package 204A	+ 1537
Whitewalls	+ 69
Cassette	+ 116
Clearcoat paint	+ 155
Subtotal	$13,105
Advertising & finance	+ 196
Subtotal (*invoice cost*)	$13,301
Pack	+ 150
Total (dealer cost)	**$13,451**

We have also looked over the newspaper ads and discovered that Ford is offering $600 cash back on Tauruses. Mmmm, goody. Since the budget is a little tight, we'll put the rebate down on the car, lowering the acquisition cost by $600. And, finally, we have calculated a range of lease payments, starting at about $1,200 under cost and going up to sticker plus 10%.

Imagining myself to be us, out I went.

A QUICK PRICE QUOTE

It was a cold, gray day, with scattered snow flurries: your basic slow day at the car store. I parked next to a little pile of snow and went into the showroom. And there was a Taurus with all the right equipment: $15,326.

A young man, around twenty-two, walked up to me and introduced himself. He was wearing a white shirt with big, bold stripes and a short-pointed spread collar. His tie was a hair wider than the stripes on the shirt. He seemed like a nice guy.

I said I liked Tauruses and was thinking about buying or leasing one. What would it cost to lease a car like the one sitting right there?

He didn't know, he said, because he was new on the job. But he did know leasing was a great way to go. He said it would save me an awful lot of money.

I knew he was supposed to check with a manager before

quoting any numbers. So I asked him if he could find out what it would cost to lease a car like this.

He said that, well, you have to have a specific car in mind. I told him, this one right here will do just fine. (You may have to walk the lot to find one like the one you want. If so, do it.) I told him that, except for the color, this one was exactly like the one I wanted. What would it cost to lease it?

He dodged the question, asking if I was ready to do a deal today. No, I was just shopping around, trying to find out about leasing and what it would cost. In fact, what would it cost to lease a car exactly like this one here? Could he find out for me?

In dodging my questions, he was merely doing his job. Handing out prices to wandering shoppers is precisely what salespeople are not supposed to do. But since I kept pressing him, he went off to talk to a manager. I stared at the Taurus.

When he came back, he tried another dodge. He said he couldn't find the right person. This was pure bull.

I said, "But I have to have some idea what it would cost to lease. I know all about buying, I've bought [two, five, seven cars already; pick a number that fits your age], but I have to find out what it would cost me to lease. What would it cost me to lease this car right here?"

Now if the salesperson keeps dancing and dodging, don't make the mistake of getting angry, as more than a few folks do. Instead, simply persist in being logical. Say that you want to compare leasing and buying. But how can you compare them if you don't know what it would cost to lease the car you want? You can't, that's how. So you need—not "want"—you "need," or "have" to know what it would cost to lease the car.

In this case, after I repeated that basic message once again, he said, "Oh, about two-fifty a month."

As you can see, the right person had been there and had given the salesman a number. But he had also given him an order not to mention the number unless he had to.

Now we compare $250 with the figures we've compiled. Cost with pack is $13,451. I added $400 for profit, so sell price is

$13,851. Subtracting the $600 rebate put down on the car leaves an acquisition cost of $13,251. Using a residual of $5,700, and a 10% lease rate, I calculated the payment several ways and came up with a range of $237 to $245.

So $250 a month is a ballpark figure that's not too bad. There may be too much profit in there ($500 to $600 instead of the $400 I used) but not a lot too much. Now we have a price and we've had a little practice at extracting information from a car salesman who didn't want to give it. And—a couple of pluses: (a) Even though he tried to withhold information, he was a pleasant enough guy; (b) his price was not an insult. In fact, it was low enough to indicate a willingness to deal. These pluses add up to a car store that deserves careful consideration, and perhaps a return trip. Mission accomplished.

A LEASE STORE

Unlike dealerships, you can shop lease stores over the phone. So I got out the Yellow Pages and called a few. Two of them financed their own deals.

One was close to my house. The guy told me he'd been in business for 20 years. I drove by the place. It was big for a lease store, as big as a small dealership, and it had a service garage. These were all positive signs. If I had been after a car, I would have gone in and done some dickering.

But one of the other places was, amazingly, a bank.

Some background: When the manufacturer's credit arms went aggressively after lease business, many banks folded their tents and went quietly back to mortgages. But in Philly, a big, old, "reputable" bank, which we'll call Third Bank, went whole hog after leasing. The bank not only finances deals for dealers and lease stores, it also runs its own in-house lease store. We'll call it BankLease.

A bank-owned lease store was new to me, so I paid them a visit. No store, no lot, no garage. Just an office in a midrise bank building plopped down in the middle of a suburban parking lot. They gave me a brochure.

THE BROCHURE

Brochures, as you know, are not textbooks. They are ads.

But despite all my warnings about ads, I was sucked in.

The brochure compared a three-year buy and a three-year lease on a car priced at $12,500. It assumed that the customer paid the 6% sales tax in cash. No other downstroke. The amount financed was $12,500.

The finance rate on the buy was 11.25%. Payment was $410.72 a month for 36 months.

The 36-month lease payment was $231.13. Plus $13.87 a month for tax.

On a three-year lease! What a deal! What an incredible deal. I couldn't see how they did it.

With a hefty discount, this twelve-five car should be the equivalent of, say, a $14,000 Taurus or Cutlass, something like that. That's a lot of car for $245 a month: You are, after all, getting the car's best years.

I mean, our $8,000 Escort cost $217 a month on a *four*-year buy. (Remember, the shorter the term, the higher the payment.)

I felt a rush of desire. I actually thought, maybe I'll go get this car.

Then, calming down a little, I decided to see if such a good deal were possible. Figuring out a 36-month lease payment on a $14,000 Taurus negotiated down to a $12,500 price, I came up with a payment about $40 a month over BankLease's. Hmmm.

I tried some lower lease rates—all the way down to 7% on Ford Credit's lease charts, and I went back to the October charts for a higher residual value—and I still couldn't get down as low as $231 a month for 36 months.

Suspicion arose. Perhaps I was in the presence of a magic

payment on a mystery car with a magnificent residual: bait to prime me for the switch.

How could they pull it off? By basing the example on a car that will have a 55% residual value after three years. The charts used would have to be October charts, in other words, the charts in use at the very beginning of the model year, not the calendar year.

Even in the beginning of the model year, few vehicles carry three-year residuals of 55%. On BankLease's charts, the highest three-year residuals I can find are a Honda Prelude at 56%, a couple of Honda Accords at 55%, a Toyota Camry at 55%, BMW's 325ic convertible at 54%, a couple of Acuras at 53%, Ford's Aerostar at 52%, Chevy's Astro Passenger Van at 51%, Dodge's Caravan at 50%. For most cars the 36-month residual, even in October, is between 39% and 47%.

To give you a little more context, on BankLease's October charts, most BMW's (a car supposed to hold its value extremely well) have three-year residuals of 45% to 47%, well under the percentage needed to attain the low payment advertised in the brochure.

If you went to BankLease for a car, your chances of matching the deal in the ad would be about one in a hundred. But the ad was a triumph. It achieved the ultimate goal of all car ads—in fact, of all advertising. It provoked intense desire. It was thoroughly misleading. It could not be proved false.

Lorna

To see how the bank explained the ad, I called them up. I asked what kind of car the example was based on.

"It's not based on any car," said a woman, whom we'll call Lorna.

"What do you mean? It has to be based on something."

"Well, it's based on an abstract car. It's, like, an example."

"Oh," I said.

"But if you tell me what kind of car you're looking for, I can work out a real price for you," she said.

So I described the fifteen-three Taurus.

"I'll call you back," said Lorna.

Next day, she did.

She quoted me a four-year lease payment of $261.92, including 6% tax. The deal allowed 15,600 miles per year, or 62,400 miles over the four years. Penalty for excessive mileage was 8¢ a mile.

I had my calculator handy, and simply by dividing 1.06 into the payment figured out that the before-tax payment for the car was $247.09 per month.

Then I asked what price the payment was based on. And Lorna gave me quite a rundown. Compare this with what you are told when you ask the same question.

Lorna told me that MSRP was $15,826 and there was a $500 package discount, so retail on the car was $15,326.

Dealer cost, she said, was $13,340. This was about right. I didn't ask if BankLease got a fleet discount—or who was pocketing it if they did. You should ask this, however.

To the $13,340, $75 was added for profit, bringing the deal price or sell price up to $13,415. Then Ford's $600 cash rebate was figured in as a down payment and subtracted, leaving an acquisition cost of $12,815. The residual value was $5,870, which also served, said Lorna, as the guaranteed buyout at the end of the lease.

The quoted price struck me as extremely good. The payment I wasn't sure about yet. I asked about the lease rate, and Lorna told me it was 9.14%.

"That sounds pretty good," I said.

"It *is* good," said Lorna. "It's the best deal you can get. No dealer will sell you a car like that for seventy-five over cost."

True enough. "I'll call you back," I said.

Checking the Payment

I talked to Lorna in January, and since I happened to have Ford's January charts, I used them first to check Lorna's payment quote. Ford pegged the Taurus's 48-month residual at 36%, a bit lower than BankLease. Then I called a Ford dealer and found the current Ford Lease rate was 9.5%.

As Lorna said she had done, I used the rebate as a down payment, resulting in an acquisition cost of $12,815. I figured residual value at 36% of $15,826, or $5,697.

With these figures and Ford charts, I calculated a payment of $234.98 per month before tax, or $250.38 after tax.

Despite a lower residual value and a lease rate almost half a percent higher, the Ford Credit payment came to $12 less than BankLease's. Something was funny.

Now, what Lorna said about the price was true. No dealer will sell you a $15,000 car for $75 over cost.

So I added $325, to bring the profit up to $400, which quite a few dealers will accept. Price is now $13,740, and acquisition cost (after subtracting the $600 down) is $13,140. Now the payment came out to $243.41, or $258.01 with tax.

That price was $325 higher than BankLease's. Yet the payment calculated with Ford charts—not the lowest around by any means—was three dollars a month lower than BankLease's.

Maybe I was making a mistake. To check my figures, I used the price at $400 over and calculated a payment with the bank method.

The acquisition cost after the rebate is still $13,140, but now I added a $200 bank fee, making it $13,340.

Using BankLease's residual value of $5,870, and a higher money factor of .00425 (a lease rate of 10.2%), I came up with a payment of $237.26 a month, or $251.50 with tax.

Again, a higher price and a higher rate than BankLease's, yet a payment of $9.83 less. How could these payments be lower than Banklease's, given BankLease's phenomenal price and rate?

Next, I tried the numbers Lorna quoted, using the basic

method. As mentioned, lenders often find this method a bit too basic and add money here and there; your use of it, however, will give you an idea of how much has been added.

Sell price	$13,415.00
Cash down	− 600.00
Acquisition cost	$12,815.00
Residual value	− 5,870.00
Depreciation	$ 6,945.00
Monthly depreciation *payment*	$ 144.69 ($6,945 ÷ 48)
Acquisition cost	$12,815.00
Residual value	+ 5,870.00
Total money	$18,685.00
Money factor	× .0038
Interest	$ 71.00
Monthly lease payment	$ **215.69** (depreciation + interest)

Thirty-one and change under BankLease's payment. What was going on?

Well, they could be lying about the price of the car. Or they could be finagling numbers around so they can misrepresent the price without really lying. Remember, in the Age of the Image, lies are not what they once were. There is only representation, and representation is the play of light on water in fog.

How to Find Out Why the Payment Does Not Match Your Calculations

You should check and verify all of the following—but if it grows too tediously involved, skip to "Lorna Spills the Beans" (page 124) for a vague but wonderful explanation.

Get Additional Information

I called Lorna and told her it seemed like I would be paying too much money. Then asked what I was paying off.

"It doesn't work that way," she said.

"How does it work?"

"Leasing gives you a low monthly payment," she said. "If you were buying the car you would be paying—"

"I know, I know," I said, "but what am I paying off?"

Now Lorna grew firm. Stern, even.

"You," she said, "are not 'paying off' like you would pay off the principal on a loan. You are paying depreciation plus interest."

"How much depreciation and how much interest?" I said.

She told me $171.70 depreciation and $75.39 interest. $171.70 + 75.39 = 247.09, sure enough. That added up okay. But some other things didn't.

Breaking Down the Payment

Let's take a look at the depreciation.

After 48 months (48 × $171.70) total depreciation paid would be $8,241.60. For convenience sake, I'll drop the change.

If the acquisition cost is $12,815 and we pay off $8,241 in depreciation, then the residual should be $4,574, not $5,870. Should it not? Does not $12,815 − $8,241 = $4,574?

To put it the other way, if the acquisition cost is $12,815 and the residual is $5,870, then the depreciation should be $6,945. Over a period of 48 months, the monthly depreciation should be $144.69, as we saw in the payment calculation, not $171.70.

I called Lorna again and told her exactly that. Then said, "If I pay $8,241 depreciation, with a residual of $5,870, I'm paying $14,111 for the car. What's going on? I thought I was getting it for $12,815."

(Plus the $600 rebate from Ford, don't forget, which is going down on the car.)

"It doesn't work that way," said Lorna. "You are getting the car for $12,815. Leasing doesn't work on an APR basis."

Lorna showed the dodges of a born car saleswoman. Here, she

was answering a customer's question with an answer to a different question.

I reminded her that I had just figured it out on a depreciation basis, not an APR basis (as you would figure out a loan).

"Oh," she said, "right. The buyout does seem a little high."

"A little?"

"Well, maybe almost a thousand dollars. I'll check with the little wizards with the computers who figure out the lease payments and get back to you."

Wizards? Computers? Golly. I felt threatened. To make sure I hadn't bollixed up the numbers, I asked what interest rate she was using.

"Nine-point-one-four," she said. "That works out to a money factor of thirty-eight."

True enough. As you recall, the money factor equals half the monthly interest rate. .0914 per year = .0076166 per month, divided by 2 = .0038083. Or, .0914 divided by 24 = .0038083.

Interest or Lease Charges

Okay, we found something peculiar, maybe even a little fishy: According to one set of Lorna's numbers, we should pay off $6,945 in monthly depreciation payments of $144.69. According to Lorna, however, we are paying $171.70 monthly depreciation.

Plus $75.39 in interest. How does that number check out?

To generate the interest payment, we take the total money subject to lease charges, or acquisition cost plus residual value, and multiply it by the money factor.

$$
\begin{array}{r}
\$12,815 \\
+\ 5,870 \\
\hline
\$18,685 \\
\times\ .0038 \\
\hline
\$71.0003 \text{ or } \$71.00
\end{array}
$$

There's something a little strange about the interest payment, too. At $75.39, it's $4.39 too much. Where do these discrepancies come from?

Three Possibilities

1. A higher acquisition cost.

Plugging an acquisition cost of $14,090 into the basic lease payment calculation yields a depreciation payment of $171.25, an interest payment of $75.85, and a lease payment of $247.10. After adding back the $600 rebate, the sell price would be $14,690.

Would BankLease quote a sell price of $13,415 while actually charging $14,690? Maybe. Some lenders do this and legitimize it through semantics. The dealer cost of the car becomes "selling price." A chosen markup, from $1,000 to as much as $1,700 in one case I've seen, is called "dealer prep," or "acquisition fee." This second amount is added to the "selling price" to reach the acquisition cost on which the lease payment is based.

2. BankLease's computer program may lower the residual when calculating depreciation and jack it up when computing interest. If so, $4,574 would be used to calculate depreciation and $7,024 to calculate interest.

How do we arrive at $7,024? By reversing the operation that yields the interest payment: the same way you solve for the principal on a loan. Dividing the interest payment Lorna quoted, $75.39, by the money factor of .0038 gives $19,839.47. Rounding off the pennies then subtracting the stated acquisition cost gives the residual: $19,839 − $12,815 = $7,024.

This possibility would give precisely the depreciation and interest payment amounts that Lorna quoted. And it would make everything slightly unreal. Simply charging a higher price could become unpleasantly real if a customer complained on the Consumer Corner of the local TV news. So my suspicion is that calculating a lease payment with two different residual values is the true function of the little wizards and their computer.

3. BankLease may simply use a lower residual all the way around.

To figure out what that number may be we need a starting point. To find one (a) use a financial calculator to solve for residual value by keying in the payment. Or (b) figure out how much money the bank must make in order for the deal to make sense. Assuming we don't have a financial calculator, doing (b) is easy. We simply compare earnings from two uses of the bank's money and come up with an amount we might call the "minimum acceptable profit"—because if the bank made less, they'd have no reason to lease cars.

If you borrowed $12,815 at the going rate to buy the car, what would the bank earn in interest?

The "going rate" rate we've been using is 10.5%; the 48-month factor for it is .0256. Multiply $12,815 by .0256 to get the monthly payment for a 48-month loan: $328.06. To get the total of the payments, multiply $328.06 by 48: $15,746.88, or $15,747. (Interest earned is $15,747 − $12,815 = $2,932.)

Now total up the lease payments: $247.09 × 48 = $11,860.32, or $11,860. Subtract that from what the bank would make on the installment loan: $15,747 − $11,860 = $3,887. To match the earnings on the loan, the bank would need $3,887 from the Taurus.

Now we plug this $3,887 into the basic method of payment calculation. A $12,815 acquisition cost, $3,887 residual, 9.14% lease rate, and a .0038 money factor yield a 48-month lease payment of $249.46 a month.

We are in the ballpark, are we not?

Adding $100 to the residual brings us to $3,987 and yields a payment of $247.77. Now we've left the ballpark and are right next door. After a few more tries, I found that a residual of $4,034 gave a lease payment of $247.10. Eureka!

Or perhaps I should say, "Eureka, sort of." For I could find no single residual value amount that gave precisely the combination of depreciation and interest payments that Lorna quoted. This reinforces my liking for possibility Number 2. But no matter how BankLease's computer calculates payments, we can say that the effective residual value in the deal is $4,034.

If selling price or residual value are different than stated, is somebody lying? Well, not exactly. You see, the lender/lessor can simply say, "We don't use them to compute the payment. We use something else."

We have seen what that something else might be in the case of the selling price. With the residual, it may be something quite simple, like "estimated future wholesale value."

BankLease's deal shows in detail how the official residual value amount may function as your guaranteed buyout but differ considerably from what I'll call the real residual: the amount used to compute the lease payment.

Why is it done this way? To allow the lender to make as much money as possible on "big" deals, while at the same time covering itself on average deals.

Lease profits come mainly from the money brought in by selling cars turned in when leases expire. But it's almost impossible to estimate what these cars will actually bring in, because the spread in the retail prices of used cars of the same make and model is enormous, as much as $3,000.

Most cars, of course, will be average. The sensible thing to do to cover oneself, then, is to base the lease payment on an estimate of a car's wholesale value in average condition. Such a payment is designed to bring in enough money so that the bank can sell most cars quickly, at wholesale prices, and still make an acceptable profit.

However, the possibility of selling a nice car for a nice, fat retail price—thousands over the wholesale price—always exists. The lessor does not want to let that fat price and that big, fat potential profit get away.

So your guaranteed buyout will be set on the assumption that your car will be nice when you turn it in. It will be set at a price the lessor hopes to receive for a nice car, not the one it must receive to make a profit.

As a result, if you want the car, you pay the piper.

Not only that, but if you have a nice, clean, low-mileage car, it will not be easy for you to make money by selling it yourself. Your nut, your payoff to the lessor, will be high. Thus the lender has a better chance of getting back that nice, clean car—and a better chance of taking the profit.

Lorna Spills the Beans

As I was cogitating about all this, time was going by and Lorna hadn't got back to me with an answer from the little wizards. This was the first time she had failed to call back when she said she would. Finally, I called her.

I said the buyout was too high for the payment, and vice versa, then asked what was going on.

Again, she began comparing leasing to buying, and I said that I understood all that.

Again, she said that leasing couldn't be calculated on an APR basis, and, again, I said I was using the depreciation basis.

Then I asked what the wizards had told her.

She said, "Huh?"

I reminded her that she was going to ask the guys with the computers why the buyout was too high.

Now, she remembered. In fact, she did go to see the wizards. But they hadn't got back to her. And now (she fussed around with something on her desk for a moment), now she couldn't find my file.

Never before had Lorna failed to find my file.

I did a little dance. I told her how helpful she was, how nice it was to deal with her, what a great deal BankLease offered, how much I wanted the car—but. But I had to have—absolutely had to have—the answers to these questions. (Remember that; it's an easy dance to learn.)

Then she said, "Oh, now I remember. There was a difference of a thousand dollars on the buyout."

"It was more than that," I said.

"No, I think it was a thousand. Let me go check."

She put me on hold and went off once more to visit the wizards.

When she returned, she apologized all over the place and told me how embarrassed she was that she had forgotten about this. However, the reason why things didn't jibe was, as she put it, "The fact of the matter is that the computer added a thousand dollars in programmed profit structure.

"And that," she said, "accounts for the difference."

"A thousand where? In the payments, or the buyout?"

"In the overall," she said. "It's part of the computer program."

I asked if it could be negotiated out of the program.

No, it couldn't.

And there you have it, a wonderful, truly modern explanation of hidden charges: "programmed profit structure . . ." Profit is no longer part of the price, like your boring, old-fashioned, run-of-the-mill-type profit, no. Now, profit is part of the program.

How Many Beans Are We Talking Here?

Had Lorna said the residual was $4,034, I would want the option to buy the car at the end of the lease for $4,034. But as we saw, the bank wants to reserve potential profit for itself. How much is that potential? How does the bank make out on a lease as compared to a buy?

Here are some approximate numbers. They don't take selling costs into account, but if the bank either wholesales the car or sells it to you, those costs will be next to zero.

Lending you $12,815 for 48 months at 10.5% would earn the bank $2,932 in interest.

Leasing you the Taurus at $75 over its cost would require an investment of $12,740. You pay $247.09 48 times for a total of $11,860.32. Let's suppose that the sale of the four-year-old Taurus will bring from $3,000 to $6,000 depending on its condition.

If the car brings $3,000, the total revenue is $14,860. The bank makes $2,120, about $800 less than it would on the loan.

If $4,000, the approximate residual, the total is $15,860. The bank makes $3,045, about $100 more than on the loan.

If $5,000, the total is $16,860, for a $4,120 return and an increase of almost $1,200 over the profit on the loan.

If you buy the car for $5,870, the total is $17,730 and the return is $4,990, more than $2,000 over the earnings on the loan. This is why banks accept the extra risk of leasing.

WHAT DOES ALL THIS MEAN TO YOU?

If you understand the inner workings of the deal, that is, the lessor's profit expectations, you understand the spread or range within which you may be able to negotiate the lease-end purchase price.

Was BankLease's Deal a Good Deal? And How Can You Tell?

The payments we have compared to BankLease's have been all over the lot: $3 lower, $10 lower, $18 lower. Given that, and given the various methods of payment calculation, how would you decide whether or not you had a good deal going?

You would make the comparisons a little differently. We have been concerned mostly with the internal consistency of Bank-Lease's arithmetic; you would be concerned with the marketplace. It is the local marketplace that ultimately determines a good deal, not arithmetical consistency. For example, you would:

- Go back to cost. With finance charges included it was $13,451. Round it off: $13,450.
- Get a realistic sell price. Add $400: $13,850.
- Subtract the rebate of $600: $13,250.

- Find out the manufacturer's estimate of residual value. In this case it's $5,670. Use that.
- Determine the low average lease rate in your market. Here, 10%.
- Inflate your price a little, since so many lenders do. Here we'll do it by adding a bank fee of $200, bringing the acquisition cost to $13,450.
- Calculate the lease payment, using the depreciation method. With the money factor for 10% rounded up to .0042, the payment is $242.38. This is your basic good deal.
- Calculate a payment without the bank fee: $237.37. Are you likely to find a deal that good? No, not in the market here. In your market, it may be possible, so be aware of it. A lender new in the market, looking for business, might offer a deal that good.
- Calculate a third payment using the method of the manufacturer's lease program. Find out what it is at a car store. Here, with our present acquisition cost of $13,250, it would be $246.72.
- Shop. Look for $240 a month before taxes while being aware that it's a super price and will be hard to find. Keep in mind that anything between $240 and $245 will be pretty good. And when you start shopping, let the salespeople know that you have in mind a deal around $235.

BankLease's deal, then, despite the discrepancies, despite the fact that its terrific rate and selling price made the image much better than the reality, was still not really that bad. It was a little high, but not a killer. And it could probably be beaten.

Because the deal wasn't bad and could probably be beaten, it would provide an extremely powerful bargaining tool, a bargaining tool which would probably make it easy for us if we actually were out to lease the Taurus. We'd simply go back to Skinny Tie and tell him we needed to beat a deal for $242 a month. And we'd like to do business with him. So . . . what could he do for us?

And if you lived in an area where car stores were scarce and all run by folks who think discounts are a Communist plot, you could do BankLease's deal and not get murdered. And, despite what Lorna said, when you got off the phone and went into the office, you might be able to talk them down a couple of dollars.

The Taurus is a lot of car for the kind of money we've been talking about. The low payments came from (a) early charts, giving high residual values, (b) a rebate, and (c) a huge discount. We started with a large package discount of $500, we negotiated, or assumed we did, a store discount of fourteen to fifteen hundred, and we used Ford's $600 rebate as cash down.

THIS IS THE KEY TO GETTING A GOOD LEASE DEAL: EARLY CHARTS AND BIG DISCOUNTS, WHICH MAKE THE MSRP—AND THEREFORE THE RESIDUAL VALUE—HIGH IN RELATION TO THE ACQUISITION COST

A BAD DEAL AT A FORD STORE

Would it really be as easy as it seemed in the last couple of sections? There's a good chance it would, because all of it actually happened. But, then again, perhaps not. In any case, I don't want to tell you it will be easy; I want to show you that you can do it, whether it's easy or not. So instead of going back to see Skinny Tie, I went to another Ford store.

Following my own advice, I went to a big one, close to home. And, even though I know what I'm doing—with this stuff, anyway—I got jerked around all over the place.

The store was H & H Ford, in the suburbs. Because you can be sued for telling unpleasant truths, let me add that this is a fictional name; that Ford Motor Company does not own this store or any car store I mention, nor does Ford control the stores' behavior; and that the things that happened at H & H happen at dealerships selling all brands of cars.

First, I called and talked to a saleswoman named Josie. She said she'd give me a great deal. I said that was what I wanted and that I'd ask for her when I came in.

When I got there, Josie was busy. I took a stroll around the lot to look at the Tauruses.

And immediately noticed a little sticker on the back window of every car. It said that the dealer had added a protection package composed of rustproofing, paint sealant, and fabric guard. The price of this package was $600.

I peered up under the wheel wells of a couple of cars; I found a car whose hood was partly open, and lifted it. And on all of them I saw . . . the yellowish goop. Rustproofing had been sprayed on all the cars.

Bingo! Red flag Number 1. If I had been in the market for a car, I would have left immediately. But since I was in the market for research, I looked over the Tauruses.

Nothing quite matched what I wanted. The closest was stock number D1516, a silver metallic number that had a power passenger seat and a couple of other options I wouldn't want enough to pay for. The car wore a sticker price of $15,873. H & H's add-on package brought the total to $16,473.

Inside the store, I found Josie. We went into her office and sat down. She asked if I had found anything I liked.

I mentioned D1516, and said it was close, but had more options than I needed and it cost too much.

"Don't worry about that," said Josie. "We'll work out a nice payment for you."

"A nice payment." What does this nice payment do? Say "please" and "thank you," and keep in mind the feelings of others? Nice? In a car store 400 long, cold miles from this place I had learned that very phrase. And many others Josie used. All over the land, the same phrases are said in the same tones of reassurance.

Next, I asked about the dealer-added protection or "pro" package, saying I didn't want it and wasn't going to pay a nickel for it.

"Don't worry about it," said Josie. "I'll get it for you for free."

What a deal, right?

Wrong. So I kept complaining about it and said I wanted a car without the package. Josie said that would be impossible. The owner put the protection package on every car as soon as it came off the truck.

"He's a thick-headed, old-fashioned German," she said.

The owner's inner nature and ethnic heritage had little to do with the rustproofing package. Josie was using the "it's-you-and-me-against-the-bad-guys" ploy. I was supposed to feel that she was my ally against the horrible old owner.

Then she told me again not to worry about the protection package, because she knew she could get it for me for free.

"I got the manager to give it to my last customers," she said. What a gal, right?

Wrong. This is an apparent discount of $600 that represents around $200 in hard dollars. That's not much on an Escort and nothing on a $15,000 Taurus.

So I changed the subject and asked how much a lease payment would be on the silver Taurus that listed for fifteen-eight.

Josie didn't like that subject, so she changed the subject herself. She asked what car it was.

I said it was the silver Taurus two cars in from the fence.

She asked if I was sure.

Was I sure?

In this world, how can one be sure of anything? Maybe I saw it in Arkansas. Maybe I saw it in a dream.

With her question, Josie was trying to do two things. One, introduce doubt into my mind, plant the idea that I might be wrong. Two, take control of the conversation by forcing me to answer silly questions. And the first objective of that control was to steer me away from the subject of money till Josie had found out more about me.

"Let me go get the stock number and the invoice," she said. "That way, we'll know what we're talking about."

She went away and was gone a long time.

When she came back, she had an invoice, or more accurately, part of an invoice. The outer and bottom edges, which bear the cost figures, had been folded under, then a copy made of the remainder, which showed only the retail figures.

Handwritten on the invoice was the stock number, D1516. I glanced at it and handed it back to her.

"This is the wrong invoice," I said.

"No, no," says Josie. She is sure it's the right one. She points out the stock number.

I point out the price. List price on the invoice—without dealer addenda—was $16,269, after an options discount of $400. But list price on the car's window sticker was $15,873, after an options discount of $500. Josie was showing me a fake invoice, hoping I hadn't paid much attention to the window sticker.

Josie said I must be mistaken, she was sure this was the right invoice: Here was the stock number and everything.

I repeated the point about the price and pointed out the difference in the Ford package discounts.

We argued about this for a few minutes. Josie kept repeating that it must be the right invoice because it had the same stock number on it.

Note that we actually argued about this.

Finally, I told her to go look at the car. She went away again. When she came back she was full of apologies. She blamed the mistake on the office staff.

"The girl," she said, "must have put the stock number on the wrong invoice."

The girl hadn't done any such thing. The VIN numbers (serial numbers) on both invoices had been the same. The one Josie showed me was a fake.

Look closely at and remember what is written on the window sticker of the car you want. Burn those numbers into your brain. Window stickers come from the factory, and it is against the law to alter or leave them off the automobile.

After Josie got done apologizing for "the girl's" mistake, I asked again what it would cost per month to lease that car.

Josie changed the subject again, then asked me for the third or fourth time how much I could afford to pay per month.

I hadn't answered—and don't you answer—this question up till now. If the salesperson presses you for an answer, say, "Afford? I can afford this car if I get a good deal, that's what I can afford."

But now, after the dealer addenda and the phony invoice, I had had enough. To be able to show you how this game works, I told Josie I could afford about $300 a month.

Then she asked me how long a lease I wanted. I told her four years.

"Oh," she said, looking concerned, "I think we're looking at five years, here."

No, I told her, I was interested in four years.

"Well, she said, "let me go have the manager put it on the computer and see what it comes to."

Away she went, again. When she returned, she was carrying a piece of computer paper. She handed it to me. The faint dot-matrix printing said:

Financial Plan For:
D1516
"B" Executive Lease

Payment schedule:
59 at	$ 300.00 + tax

Cash required:
1st Pmt	318.00
Sec Deposit	518.00
License Fee	80.00
Prepayment	38.16
Tax on Prepay	0.00
TOTAL	$ 954.16
Residual	$5,000.00

That's it, verbatim. Computerized compost.

Consider: If I negotiated a $1,200 discount (leaving $800 for profit) and put down Ford's cash rebate, I could buy the car on a Ford Credit 10.9% sixty-month loan for $318.51 a month including tax. Here was a lease payment the same as a buy payment on a deal that was only halfway decent.

Consider: On a 48-month lease, you pay about $2.50 more per month for every $100 in increased cost. At $15,873 plus, say, $300 for the pro package, this car listed for $847 more than BankLease's.

At $2.50 per hundred, that's 8.47 times $2.50 = $21.18.

$247 (BankLease's payment) + $21 = $268; $268 and change per month (before tax) for 48 months.

H & H, however, was asking $300 for 60 months: $5,100 more than I needed to pay. Of course, I have to admit that eventually Josie would have knocked that payment down by about $25 a month. And I would have paid only $3,600 more than necessary.

And, finally, consider: After years in the car business, I had never before seen the "prepayment" that popped up in H & H's "Financial Plan." Maybe it was what I had to pay to round off the numbers. More likely, it wasn't anything but a little ripoff added to a big ripoff. If it were a payment for something, it would have been taxed.

H & H's Price

Using charts from three different lenders and a lease rate of 10.2% (money factor of .00425), I can't make a 60-month lease payment on a $15,873 car with a $5,000 residual value come out to $300 a month. Not even at sticker price plus $600 for add-ons.

The best I could do, using the phony invoice price of $16,269, then adding $600 for the "protection package" and another $200 for a bank fee, was just under $295 a month.

The lease payment Josie handed me for a car that retailed at fifteen-eight was based on a price of about seventeen-three to seventeen-four. How about that?

Now, how about this: Some car stores follow a practice of basing the first quoted lease payment on sticker price plus 5% to 10%.

H & H's Payment Strategy

Josie and her boss followed a script that might be called *Kick 'Em, Then Kiss 'Em While They're Crying*. Here's how it goes. It may happen to you.

They whack me with the $318 payment. Thinking I can't afford the car, I feel humiliated, afraid, angry.

All of a sudden, Josie sees the light. The manager, that dirty dog (at this point, you see, it's her and me against the manager) forgot to take off the $600 for the dealer-added package. She goes back to him. And comes back with a payment reduced by, say, $12.72, to $305.28 a month.

"There, that's better, isn't it, Mike?"

No. I can only afford $300 a month, no higher.

Away she goes again and back she comes with another reduction. Say, $297.94, with a $42 "prepayment."

"There," she says, "I really had to fight for you, Mike. I mean, I stuck up for you so much that my manager got mad at me. But now he'll lease you the car for $297.94, and that includes taxes. That's a hell of a deal. A really nice payment for you, Mike. A really good deal. Here, give me your okay right down here before he changes his mind."

If I object, she'll tell me that the new payment was twenty a month less, a $1,200 discount. She not only got me the protection package for free, she got the manager to take off another $600!

This new figure represents a 60-month payment of $281.08 and a price of about $16,200. In other words, sticker, plus add-ons, minus a $200 discount on the add-ons. And a profit of $2,600 or thereabouts.

The add-on package, whether a protection package or a prettification package (a decor group) will have a retail price around three times its actual cost. Both the package and the payment strategy are designed to make you think you are getting a major discount while you buy the lease at sticker or sticker plus.

And when the salesperson asks how much you can afford per month, this is the scene she is setting for you. Your role is Prize Sucker.

Psywar: The Strategy Behind Josie's Sales Technique

In support of the payment strategy is an attempt to confuse you, wear you out, and make you doubt yourself and your idea of a good deal. To accomplish this, salespeople wage psychological warfare.

Every assertion you make is challenged. Every time you say something, the salesperson contradicts you—even if they fully intend to agree with you and apologize later. Then, after a little argument, the salesperson leaves to check on something—and is gone a long time. You sit and wait and stew. Then the salesperson returns with a document.

The meaningless arguments and the irritation and boredom of waiting are intended to drain your energy, to wear you down before beginning the negotiation for dollars.

The (slightly) more meaningful arguments, coupled with the documents—and computerized documents at that—are meant to insinuate doubt. The salesperson's message is: "I am in the business; I have the invoice [but not the cost figures]; I have the computer; you don't have any of that so you must be wrong, especially about your idea of a good deal."

The theory is that once you begin to doubt yourself, you begin to suspect that the salesperson is right. After all, she is in the business. Maybe you made a mistake somewhere.

What comes next is the basic propaganda technique known as the big lie. The salesperson will insist, over and over, that, in fact, they are right, that you are getting a good deal, that if they could lease you the car for any less they would do it in a minute. After all, they are there to sell cars, aren't they? Doesn't that make sense? They are *desperate* to sell cars. If there were any way they could do what you want, they'd do it without another word.

Now, according to the plan, the force of repetition brings you to feel that you must be very close to getting the best deal possible. And once you reach that stage, a small but dramatic drop in the payment (dramatic because it crosses a psychological threshold), say from $300 a month to $296.80 a month, will make you feel a surge of relief. You'll think, "There, I got it." And sign. And lose a bundle.

Before taxes, $296.80 represents a lease payment of $280 a month, $5 to $7 a month more than it would cost to lease the car for 48 months with a reasonably good deal. You'd be paying an extra $5 for 48 months, or $240, plus twelve extra $280 payments or $3,360: a total of $3,600 more than necessary to lease the car for the length of time you originally wanted it, which was four years.

Alternate scenario: They pound away at you as above, but get nowhere. They decide you're a tough cookie. Instead of dropping the payment, they suddenly "realize" they've made a horrible mistake. The girl in the office pushed the wrong button on the computer. The payment is right, $300 a month plus tax, but the term really should be 48 months, not 60.

You think, "I knew it." And sign. Since the payment is $25 a month over the reasonably good deal payment of $275 for 48 months, you'd lose a mere $1,200.

If you begin to feel yourself being worn down, if you sense the onset of fatigue and doubt, leave. Even if you want to do business at that store, don't do the deal when you feel tired and weak. Walk out and come back another day.

FIVE

Games, Moves, and Attitude: Their Advantages; Your Advantages

Most salespeople are more subtle than Josie. It's unlikely that you'll encounter one who plays her game so aggressively, so go-for-broke. If you do, tell her as pleasantly as possible to cut the bullshit. Then tell her you already know you can lease the car you want for such and such a payment. And ask how much better she can do for you.

Keep your cool. Be logical and polite. And repeat yourself till you want to barf. All the people we've talked to—Skinny Tie, Lorna, and now Josie—have tried to avoid answering questions. Skinny Tie said he didn't know the answer. Lorna answered different questions and changed the subject. Josie changed the subject, started irrelevant arguments, then went away, leaving me to cool my heels.

These ploys are intended to control the flow of conversation and to withhold information. Ignore them. Ignore what you do not want to hear and repeat your statements and questions until the salesperson responds.

THE BALL

If you are looking for a mass-market car (if not, forget this particular scam) and the salesperson thinks that you're shopping around for prices, you may get a response that knocks your socks off. You may get balled.

The "ball" has little technique or strategy to it. The salesperson simply says she will lease you the car for a price so low that you cannot get it for that price anywhere on earth.

The objective is to "take you out of the market," to prevent you from doing the deal anywhere else before you come back to see the salesperson who balled you. It gives her and the store one last shot at getting your business.

Balling is sometimes referred to as highballing and sometimes as lowballing. The highball is an offer for your trade-in so far above its value that no one can match it. The lowball is an unmatchably low payment or sell price on the new car.

Whatever it's called, balling works. The main reason it works is that an unbelievable number of people try to hide the fact that they are shopping around. They tell salesperson after salesperson that he is the first salesperson they've talked to. They say, "I just want your best price. Just gimme your best price."

My best price is the most I can get out of you. If I have to give you a deal, it's the compromise I can make between you and the manager. If you've been shopping around, what I want to know is what payment will beat the other guys' and enable me to lease you the car right now, today. If you tell me what it is, I'll try to get it for you. And if I can't, I'll tell you what I can get for you.

But if you tell me I'm the first guy in a series, I'll quote you the unbeatable price. And 99% of the others will do the same. This results in customers shuffling from dealer to dealer, from ball to ball, from lie to lie. They become confused, frustrated, and angry. Then, very often, wherever they happen to be when they become so frustrated, so sick of it all that they can't stand it any longer, they do the deal. And end up not really knowing whether they got a good deal or not.

How to Dodge the Ball and Turn It to Your Advantage

If you are shopping price from store to store, simply announce what you are doing. Don't ask for a "best" price or an "honest" price. Rarely will you get it. Salespeople learn, painfully, that when let out the door with an honest price, hardly one person in ten comes back.

Instead, tell the salesperson you're trying to beat a lease payment of X based on a sell price of Y, whatever they happen to be. Make those numbers a bit lower than the best deal you think you can get. Then ask the salesperson if she can beat those numbers, and if so, by how much.

She will ask if you are ready to do the deal today. If you are, say so. If not, say so and tell her how many other prices you intend to collect. Handle this up front and swiftly.

If you say you're shopping around, she may quote a ball price to make sure you come back to her. You should—since you've done your homework—recognize immediately that it is impossibly low. Steel yourself: We all hate to admit that an impossibly low price is, in fact, impossible.

If you spot a ball price, check it. Have the salesperson go over everything with you.

Once certain that the price is too low, sign the deal. Then sit back and enjoy the movie as the salesperson wriggles and jives and tries to explain why the manager won't accept it.

This movie should have a happy ending. Once the salesperson and manager have balled you, they almost always abandon all hope for a big score. They accept the idea that you will get a good deal.

And you do get it. A manager who knows you've been shopping, believes you've been balled, and believes that you'll walk out of his store and lease the car somewhere else, feels extremely heavy pressure to take the deal away from the competition.

The pressure is so heavy that, if they don't ball you, it may be wise to make them think someone else has.

To do this, tell the salesperson that someone has promised to lease you the car for the typical ball price: cost minus freight. (Look up cost in your cost and price book. Either leave out or subtract the freight.) This price is so typical that almost everybody uses it. One reason is that freight runs $300 to $600, so a ball at cost minus freight will be well under a ball at cost minus, say, $200. And people will return first to the store that quotes the lowest price.

The other reason it's widely used is that it provides a semi-believable excuse: "Oh, jeez, I'm sorry, I forgot the freight. They keep it separate, and I'm new on the job and—"

Cost less freight is so typical that most managers—in a competitive market—will recognize it immediately as a ball, as a price someone gave you so you would not lease the car elsewhere before coming back to see them.

To make it work to your advantage, simply assert that this happened. Use the price and payment at cost without freight as your first serious offer in the negotiation.

Exception: If you want a car for which demand outruns supply, saying that you've been offered a deal at the ball price probably won't mean much.

ATTITUDE AND YOUR ADVANTAGES

At the dealership or lease store, you'll be smack in the middle of a process of action-reaction: live, unscripted theater. There are, however, a few useful guidelines and a few helpful dos and don'ts. And there are moves and maneuvers you should be able to recognize. Some of them will be tried on you.

First, about your attitude and advantages:

• Be reasonable. If you go out to get a $300 deal and wind up with one at $324, take it. Why drive around for days, suffer needless aggravation, not to mention wear and tear on your heart and stomach lining, all to save $15 to $50 on an $8,000 to $20,000 purchase?

- Be nice. I don't mean be a wimp—if the salesman gets in your face, you get in his face—just be polite and friendly. Act as if you want him to like you because you want to sell him something. Which you do. You want to sell him the idea that giving you a good deal will be a quick and painless way for him to make a little money.

    Furthermore, it may help you quite a bit later on if the salesperson's feelings about you are positive. He doesn't have to fall in love with you, just think that you are a nice enough person to recommend him to someone else—if he is nice to you. What such feelings amount to is a salesperson who will go out of their way to help you if you have trouble with your car.

- Don't play games. Don't try to talk big, don't act tough and don't poormouth.
- Allow yourself plenty of time—and take your time. Let the salesperson play her games; let her go through her routine. Don't rush things. The more time she spends with you, the more she has to lose, so the more she'll want, and need, to make a deal with you.
- Try to put yourself in the salespeople's shoes; understand their advantages over you and your advantages over them.

The people who sell cars have a certain boldness or audacity. They are not afraid to tell half-truths and outright lies—and not afraid to be caught at it. They know the numbers on the cars or can find them out easily. They have training and practice at running scams. And they have experience in high-dollar negotiations.

All of that notwithstanding, you are in control of the salesperson's most potent tools. For what salespeople use to make big scores are the customers' ignorance and emotions. When you have the handle on those things, the salesperson does not.

Replace ignorance with knowledge, keep your emotions under control, and the slickest, most skillful salesperson on the planet will have little to work with.

And most of the salespeople you meet won't be all that slick. If they were, they wouldn't be selling cars to the public. They'd be selling guided missiles or $600 toilet seats to the government. And they'd be working fewer hours, eating in much better restaurants, and making three times as much money.

So don't be intimidated.

And don't feel that you need to be hostile to keep the salesperson off balance. Hostility often doesn't work, and if it doesn't, you merely waste goodwill. And give the salesperson a motive to seek revenge, later.

There are no games or tricks or techniques of negotiation that provide you with anywhere near the power that self-control and knowledge provide.

Your Advantages Over Salespeople

Everybody in the Store Needs You More Than You Need Them A lot more. If they do not do your deal at your price, the salesperson loses the commission, the manager loses her commission, and the house loses its profit. No matter how small that commission or profit would have been, none of them can ever make it up. For there are no more you's.

There are, however, plenty of other cars at plenty of other stores. You do not lose the car. They lose and you don't. And they know it. Therefore, a salesperson would much rather give away most of the profit than lose a sale. A slice of bread is better than no loaf at all. (Always better for the salesman, not always for the manager—that is, until the end of the month rolls around.)

To show you what I mean, at the East Babbit Ford Store, a skinny little $200 deal would earn: a 25% commission on the profit, or $50; a $25 delivery fee or bonus; and done deal. Every deal brought a salesperson closer to earning the monthly bonus, which came in varying amounts depending on the number of cars sold. After a certain number, the per car amount of the bonus went up. After so many more, it went up again. If a skinny deal where I made very little money boosted me to a level where I received an extra $10 per car bonus, for, say, fifteen cars sold, that skinny little deal would earn me not only the $75 but also an extra $150 in bonus money.

There's also a boost in morale and the very real possibility that the customer will send in a friend or two, resulting in a couple more deals. You figure it out. Who needs whom? Do not feel that you are chiseling or wasting a salesperson's time by going after a good deal.

You Control the Money This seems obvious. Perhaps not so obvious is that you control it most powerfully after you've made a deposit.

When you make a written offer on a car, the offer is supposed to be accompanied by a deposit. If the deposit isn't there, the salesperson gets reamed.

Behind the demand for a deposit is a theory: Once you hand over cash, you hurdle the principal psychological barrier between you and the deal; when you hand over cash, you commit yourself to buying or leasing that car. This is supposed to, and usually does, make it easier for the salesman to "work" you, which means manipulate your emotions, and to "raise" you, or "bump" you, which mean persuade you to pay more. For once you have committed yourself, it is quite painful to be denied. But through its pricing power, the store can deny you the car. Your human need to avoid emotional pain makes you easier to manipulate.

Many customers, highly aware of this, hate to pay the deposit. But if you have control of yourself, the deposit gives you more power over them than they gain over you.

The moment you part with cash, both salesman and manager become more confident that they'll make the deal. Even though they know they shouldn't, they begin to count their chickens;

they begin spending the extra money your deal will put into their paychecks that month.

And now you have the power to take that money away from them. If that hurts them more than losing the car hurts you—if you are willing to give up the car, and your salesperson knows it—you gain an edge the moment you make a deposit.

The Walkout This is your edge in action, your ace of trumps, your killer move. It is simply the threat to leave the dealership without doing a deal. It comes in an infinite variety of shapes, forms, and intensities. And the great thing about it, as the Boss said of the lease payment, is that they (salespeople and managers) can never figure it out. They never know for certain whether or not you mean it.

For it's always an ultimatum—but never really an ultimatum until you actually get into your car and drive away. Remember, when negotiating, you can agree with anything, promise anything, threaten anything, and then take it all back in the next breath. You can walk all the way to the door (the salesman will probably follow you), then turn around suddenly and say "Hey, I like this place. Why can't I get a fair deal here?"

Or you can merely glance at your watch and stir restlessly in your chair. The saleswoman will be paying close attention to your body language. Get restless and she will start to worry.

Or, if seated, you can stand up. When a customer stands without explanation, the first thing that flashes through a salesman's mind is "Oh, shit. The guy's leaving. What did I do wrong?"

And if you walk away from the desk and wander out into the showroom, hearts will stop. For everybody in the place thinks that a customer not under complete control is a customer ready to bolt out the door. With you wandering around, even the tough-as-nails managers will feel as if the sky is falling.

After you've made the deposit, you don't even have to move. Just mutter, "I dunno. We can't seem to get anywhere. Maybe you should give my money back." Give back? Give back money? Every fiber of your salesperson's being will scream with pain.

You get the idea. The variations are endless. But employ them judiciously; don't bluff too often.

The Salesperson's Countermoves

Arguments People have heard that salespeople will not argue with them. "Win the argument, lose the sale," the saying goes. But as Josie was kind enough to show us, this ain't necessarily so.

In fact, a large part of a salesperson's skill consists of the ability to provide convincing, nonthreatening reasons why everything you say is wrong. The argument cannot become sharp enough to offend you, but because the salesperson is fighting information that you've gathered from God only knows what sources, it must be carried on in some fashion. Here are some of the points your salesperson may try to argue and win:

- The salesperson is in the business and has the facts; neither you nor anyone you have talked to really knows anything. We have seen this one in action.
- Even if you do have some knowledge, you have unknowingly made a mistake. For example, if you have a legitimate payment quote, and it's an okay deal, your salesman will not want to hear about it. So he may try to discredit it by saying it's based on a residual value from charts that are too old, or charts from the wrong lender.

  When somebody quotes you a lease payment, get all the relevant details, including name of the lender, month of the residual value charts, the factor, or percentage of MSRP being used to figure the residual, and the residual value dollar amount. With this information, you can cross-check what the next salesperson tells you.
- Similar to this is the claim that your price or payment is based on the wrong car: a car with a smaller engine or fewer options. Write things down. If you get a price quoted on a car with a

couple hundred dollars' fewer options than you want—which happens frequently—you'll drive yourself crazy trying to match or beat it on a car that has all the options.

- If you have a trade: The salesperson would pay you exactly what you want for it, except . . . Except that, unbeknownst to you, your car is one of those that is famous for needing repairs to the camshaft, or the constant velocity joints, or the computer-controlled bivalve. And that just happens to be a $500 repair, so . . .

This argument sometimes begins with a neat ploy, a game we might call "Whatever You Want, I'll Give You More." If you want $3,000 for your car, the salesperson says, "Gee. I might be able to get you close to four. Could we do business?"

You bet we could. This is an appeal to your pride and greed. The object is to stir up your emotions so the salesperson can manipulate them, then draw from you an offer and deposit: a commitment to lease the car.

Once that's done, the saleswoman begins pointing out a few of the thousand and one defects of your car, gradually hacking away at the trade allowance. All the while, she blames the manager. The manager says it needs new paint. The manager says the transmission is bad. Etc., etc. As did Josie, the saleswoman will blame anything and anyone she can think of. She agrees with you, but you are wrong. Everyone else says so.

- With leasing, you are sometimes told flat out that you don't know what you are talking about. As with Lorna's "Leasing doesn't work that way." Or "There is no price when you lease." How would you respond to the last statement?

You would say, "Sell price, minus cash down, minus trade equity, plus lender fees, plus cash owed on trade equals acquisition cost." Right?

Agreement

Agreement about important things occurs in the form of a question. If you are obviously right and the salesperson agrees with you, he may do so in the form of a question. "Well, what if it is worth three thousand? If I could get you three thousand, would you lease the car today?"

The form of that question is the master or template used to structure negotiations: "If I could . . . would you . . . ?" If I could (do whatever it is you want) would you (take the car)?

A good salesperson makes no statements. If she makes no statements, she tells no lies.

Those are a few of the more common "rational" sales games. Here are some of the emotional ones. I've listed them as dos and don'ts, mostly don'ts.

1. Don't be frightened by a payment quote way over sticker. It's supposed to frighten you, loosen up your emotions so the salesperson can calm you, soothe you, and then smooth you into paying a bunch.

2. Don't believe that salespeople who appear slow, steady, calm, and polite are therefore trustworthy. This is a common belief. It is also an expensive belief.

3. Don't believe that young, inexperienced, or clumsy salespeople will be nicer to you, or help you out or will be unable to lie effectively. This is an even more common belief.

Managers control inexperienced salespeople very closely. And they use youth and inexperience as a cover for flagrant lies, gambling that such a person will sound truthful when they say that there's only a $1,000 mark-up on a $17,000 car, or something equally ridiculous. For youth and inexperience create the illusion of innocence.

On top of that, managers will not allow new salespeople to sell a car as cheaply as experienced ones. The neophyte is being trained, and no one trains people to sell cars, or anything else, by giving away money. Once they know how to sell, or so goes the theory, they will give away money only when they have to.

4. Don't trust a salesperson who appears to be your "brother," your "sister," your "soulmate," or your "paisan."

Someone who shares your gender, your ethnic heritage, your deepest interests, or your age group and its most profound life experiences will grease you up and down and all over with this sharing. You will be slathered with it. And sharing is, indeed, wonderful. But if you allow yourself to be affected by it, the salesperson will take a larger share of your money.

5. Don't trust a salesperson because they are cute and act as if they like you, and might, if you played your cards right, do certain enjoyable things with you. The biggest score made while I was at the Ford Store came from a customer who believed this; it is the most expensive belief of all.

6. Do be careful when you are given freebies or when the salesperson agrees with you too easily. Nothing is free. Either you've already been taken for a bundle, or, perhaps, the salesperson is setting you up for the sneakiest scam of all: the phony payment scam.

This is when winning on price equals losing on payments. The salesperson simply agrees to lease you the car at the price you want, then writes in a payment which is $5, $10, or $15 a month too high.

If you catch them, it's an honest mistake. They looked at the wrong chart. Or they added in life, accident, and health insurance, which everybody wants, because something, God forbid, but something could happen to you. . . . But if you don't want it, they'll just take it right out.

If you don't catch them, everybody's happy.

Do not expect to be rescued from the phony payment scam by seeing the price on the contract. The vast majority of lease contracts contain nothing remotely resembling a price.

And do not expect to be rescued by the factory's credit company, as was my Ranger customer. All a salesman has to do to turn phony payments into sincere payments is sell you a protection package for another $1.75 a month on a "special." Who could resist? Protection from this, protection from that, protection forever, all for $1.75 a month? Nobody could resist. The huge markup on the package would then absorb the excessive charge created by the phony payment.

Do the games and scams never end? Frankly, no. But don't

worry. You can handle most of them simply by doing your homework. As for the rest, take a lesson from the salesperson's training manual. Salespeople are taught that customers lie continually. Since the lies are all part of a game, however, they should never cause the reaction they would in everyday life. Instead, they should go in one ear and out the other.

Politely ignore everything the salesperson says except what you need to hear. When he tells you which button controls the power wingding, pay attention. When he tells you what residual value and lease rate he's using, pay attention. When he explains a clause in the contract, pay attention. When he tells you that your price is way off base and gives you seven reasons why, think about a nice day at the beach.

And finally: Do expect to be treated well.

If you are not, if the salesperson is too pushy, or refuses to answer your questions, but you feel she has potential, tell her about it. If she doesn't improve, or you feel she cannot improve, leave. Salespeople are taught to put themselves in your shoes and to treat you as they would like to be treated. If they cannot master that lesson, they don't deserve your business.

THE CAR

A salesperson's goal is to increase your desire for the car while at the same time heightening your sense of urgency, till everything in you is screaming, "I want it now." So she will be sure to point out that the car is, indeed, a many-splendored thing. She will, or is supposed to, demonstrate every feature and option that makes the car valuable. The purpose is to create in your mind a concrete picture of tremendous value. For people do not do deals when they are thinking about the money they are going to spend. They do deals when they are thinking about what they are going to get. The salesperson wants to take your mind off the deal for dollars and lock it onto the deal for value.

You can use the entire routine to gain information.

- Make sure the car has the options you want—and the options the sticker says it has. Find out where all the controls are and how they work.
- As the salesperson is showing you various features, ask about how completely and how long they are covered by the warranty. Don't be shy about asking "dumb" questions. Nobody expects you to know everything about the new car.
- Check carefully for dents and scratches. Also check for misaligned body panels. Everything should look like it fits together properly. Open and close all the doors. Make sure they close easily. If they don't now, they probably never will.
- Inside the car, check for misaligned door and headliner upholstery panels. If the seams are crooked, or the pieces of cloth appear to have been put on in the dark, you're looking at a wrong car. Find another one. And if it's night, be sure to have the car pulled into the garage—the brightly lit garage. If the garage is dim, return and inspect the car during the day.
- Read the window sticker. Read it thoroughly. Check the options carefully. BURN THE MSRP, THE FACTORY DISCOUNT, AND THE STICKER PRICE INTO YOUR BRAIN. Remember, a price and package discount discrepancy was how I spotted Josie's phony invoice.
- What you can't use this routine for is to talk in any meaningful way about price or payments. Many people try, but it's a waste of time.

The Test Drive

In most stores in most areas, the test drive is an important part of the pageant of splendors: a selling tool. The salesperson wants you to feel the difference between the new car and your old rattletrap. He wants you to smell that new-car smell. He wants you to feel that smooth, tight, quiet new-car ride.

But at a few stores in some areas, test drives are discouraged. If you run into that, discourage the salesman. Convince him that you will not lease a car you cannot drive.

Then drive the car. I don't care if it's dark and snowing and you've driven 50 of the exact same model. Drive the car. Make sure everything fits and works. Make sure it accelerates, shifts, and handles properly. That the radio works, the heater works, the air works, all the power doodads work, the windshield wipers and squirters work, and so on.

Not only does this give you a chance to check out the car, but, in stores where test drives are seen as selling tools, it also makes it easier for your salesperson to handle his boss during the deal.

This is important. The salesperson will be trying to manipulate both you and the manager at the same time. No matter how much the salesperson wants to give you the deal you're asking for, his boss will be telling him to sell you the house deal. Your driving the car will make it much easier for him to sell the boss your deal.

If you don't drive it and the manager finds out—as he probably will—he'll get angry. And then he'll make an assumption. He will assume that you are making a low offer because the salesperson did not do his job. He will assume the salesman failed to whet your appetite for the car. He won't take your low offer very seriously, assuming you would have offered more had your desire been properly tweaked. Therefore, he may very possibly reject a deal he would otherwise take.

Okay, you're driving. Suppose the engine, transmission, axles, or some other part of the drive train makes funny noises? By "funny," I mean grinding, clicking, ticking, howling, or moaning noises.

Forget it. Find another one.

Suppose it runs rough? This is a judgment call. If you think the engine is running rough because of dirty plugs, or some other minor problem, it's probably worthwhile to make a contingency deal.

This means that you include a note on the purchase order saying that the deal is contingent upon the car running smoothly (or other problem being solved) when you test-drive it again before taking delivery.

Before taking delivery. Come back in a day or two and drive it. If it still doesn't run right, find another one or cancel the deal and get your deposit back. Don't take a car that the dealer has failed to fix on the first try. Don't take it even if you've already signed the lease contract. (The F & I Guy, or Business Manager, who handles financing, life, accident, and health insurance, and, increasingly, the sale of the after-sale items like rustproofing, paint gloss, etc., will try to talk you into signing the contract ahead of time. Don't do that, either.) Remember, no matter how many times a salesperson or a manager says, "You bought it, pal [or honey]," you can always cancel the deal until you actually drive that car off the lot.

SIX

Negotiating the Price

To start with, a note on terminology:

The word "price" is sometimes used as shorthand for "price and lease payment." You have to pay attention to and work with both. However, expressions like "come up $50 on the price," mean price alone. On the 48-month leases we have been using as examples, $50 in price equals about $1.25 in monthly payment.

"Raise you" and "bump you" mean persuade you to pay more. "Over," as in "$200 over" or "$900 over," means over dealer cost, which we have been defining as invoice cost plus the dealer's pack. "Under cost" means under invoice cost (without pack), unless otherwise noted.

THE PURCHASE ORDER FORM

When you sit down at the salesperson's desk, he will produce a form. This is the purchase order or purchase offer form. It is not a contract; it's more like a letter of agreement or letter of intent. When signed by the manager, however, it tends to bind the store. So, when the deal is done, make sure the manager signs that form. If he doesn't (at a few stores, not all), you leave yourself open to the "bump on delivery." In this nasty little scam, you're told you have a deal. But when you come in to take delivery, you find that they have discovered a mistake: Sorry, but they undercharged you. And now you must pay more money or you cannot have the car.

What to Have Written on the Purchase Order Form

The salesperson will write down your name, address, and phone number. He will probably write down a list of the car's equipment, and, perhaps, the sticker price.

He may, however, skip the price and write down only a lease payment, which will be based on sticker or sticker plus. It will probably be expressed like this: "Customer will lease for X months for $ X per month plus tax [plus trade, if you have one]."

That formula, "Customer will lease for a certain number of months for a certain amount plus tax [and trade]" was the way I, and everyone else at the Ford Store, expressed 99% of the lease deals we wrote. You should recognize that the formula opens your wallet for the salesperson.

Get the price—and the acquisition cost, if different—written down on the purchase order form. Never the payment alone. The payment should be expressed as a number based on a price. For example, "Customer will lease for X months for X dollars and cents per month, based on a price of X dollars and an acquisition cost of X dollars."

If you are putting money down, the purchase order should say "Based on a price of X minus Y cash down, leaving an acquisition cost of Z."

If you are trading in, it should say, "Based on a price of X minus a trade allowance of Y, leaving an acquisition cost of Z." With price, acquisition cost, and payment expressed in writing as a relationship, you will have recourse against the store should they manage to play the phony payment trick on you (see page 183).

TO DICKER OR NOT TO DICKER?

What happens next depends on your approach. You must make a choice between the direct approach and the negotiation.

I tend to agree with people whose advice is: Don't dicker. Simply announce the deal you want, and push for it until you get it. If you don't get it, walk out.

But the world is not so simple that this will always work. You may end up going to an awful lot of stores and making an awful lot of announcements. So I'll provide a method of negotiation to use as a fallback strategy should the salesperson manage to outflank the direct approach.

THE DIRECT APPROACH

Have the salesperson write the deal you want on the purchase order form in terms of price, acquisition cost, and payment. Sign it. Slap down ten or twenty bucks for the deposit. Make sure the salesperson understands that this is your offer, not a talking point. Tell him, this is it: This is as far as you go. Ignore his protestations.

But try not to be too abrupt. Sugarcoat your demands. Tell the salesperson that you want to do business with him and you are ready to do it right now, today. If he gets you your deal, it will be the quickest, easiest money he ever made. That's the benefit you are selling the salesperson: quick, easy money; no sweat, no strain.

This will be meaningful, believe me. If the salesperson has any experience at all, he will have suffered through knock-down, drag-out deals where he made no more money than you are offering for a few minutes of pleasant chat.

You may, however, encounter resistance. After all, the shortest distance between two points is the route on which your salesperson makes the least money. So he will try to turn the direct approach into a negotiation.

Resistance to the Direct Approach

Resistance will first come in the form of asking you to justify your price. The salesperson will ask, "Where in the world did you get your figures?" His tone of voice will imply you got them from outer space. Then, more seriously, he will (a) ask you to justify, that is, explain the rational basis for, your price and your payment. Or (b) he will assert that your price is impossible, that your figures are wrong.

Say that you've looked up the numbers—after all, anybody can look up the cost of a car. Then you figured out the deal you wanted. Then you went to a few places and checked: You shopped around. And you know you can lease the car for that price. If not here, then somewhere else. But you want it to be here. Because you like the place, or it's convenient for you, or because you heard they had good service.

Other Forms of Resistance

- If you have a trade, the salesperson may disagree with what you are asking for it. Say that you shopped it around and got offered X, Y, and Z. You know you can get what you're asking.
- If he agrees about the price of the car and the trade allowance but argues with your payment, say that you learned how to figure it out, then shopped around and double-checked.
- He may imply you are fibbing about your trade by asking you why you didn't take one of the other deals you were offered. Tell him that you need a car to drive: You can't sell the old one till you get a new one. And that's why you're here, with him, trading in, offering him some fast, easy money.

Give these answers once. If the salesman keeps pressing for further justification, turn the tables on him. Start asking him to justify his refusal to make the deal with you. Say, politely, that you told him where you got your numbers, and they sound like a good deal. Unless he can beat that deal. Can he? If not, why not? Why can't he do better than that for you?

Make him feel that refusing your offer will cause you to lower it, not raise it. Pound into the salesman's brain a few simple facts. One, you know what you're doing. Two, you have faith in yourself and your numbers. Three, you will not be moved: The only deal you'll take is the one you've just stated. When he is convinced of this, he'll start trying to convince the manager.

If the salesman refuses to be convinced, he's trying to get around you, to circumvent the direct approach and force you into a negotiation. Use the walkout. Start mild: Move around restlessly in your seat. Increase the intensity if necessary. The salesman will become convinced.

As you probably know, salespeople are not permitted to authorize deals. So now he'll take your deposit to the cashier and the purchase offer, or deal, to a manager. And now you will enter a form of negotiation, whether you want to or not. For few managers will accept your offer without making a few counters of their own. To stay with the direct approach, you must cut this process short.

THE MANAGER'S COUNTEROFFER

The Low Counter

If the counter is low, only a hundred or two above your offer, it usually means the manager has pretty much accepted the idea that you will get your deal, but he's duty-bound, of course, to try for another buck or two.

Just say no. Start fussing around restlessly as if getting ready to leave. Push the purchase offer toward the salesman. Say, "That's it. That's my price. Get it for me, or we can't do any business."

Repeat this either till it works, or till you become certain it will not work. At that point, ask for your deposit back.

A salesman cannot give back a deposit. He has to talk to a manager and a manager has to sign your receipt before the cashier will take the cash or check out of the till. And managers do not return deposits on the first request. They send the salesperson back with another offer. In the case of a low initial counter, the next offer will probably be what you want.

If not, tell the salesperson it's still too high and you want your money back. After going away this time, he will return with your deal or your deposit.

The High Counter

The manager may counter at a much higher price. For example, you offer $250 over dealer cost and he counters at $100 under sticker.

The manager is trying to stonewall you. Move immediately to the walkout. Tell the salesman that it looks like you can't do any business here and ask for your deposit back. He'll go back to his manager and explain that you won't budge, that you are asking for your money back, and that they have to return it to you or make your deal.

The Medium Counter—with Hammer

The manager's counter will be about halfway between sticker price and where you want to be. But with this offer, he will tell the salesperson to hammer you. The salesperson will say they simply cannot meet your figures. This new offer is the absolute lowest they can go without losing money on the deal. He will say it over and over, a dozen different ways. And it will sound like the truth.

Don't be intimidated. Instead, tell him—politely—to prove it. Tell him you want to see the invoice—the part with the cost figures, not the retail figures. Give him these alternatives: You want the deal at your price, you want your deposit back, or you want to see the cost figures on the invoice showing why he can't meet your price.

They won't want to show you the invoice. So now you'll either get your deal or get your deposit back. And leave.

If you do leave, but the place is convenient and has a good reputation, it may be worthwhile to come back the next day. Sometimes nothing short of walking out will convince a manager that you mean what you say.

When you return, ask your salesperson if his boss is going to let him do some business and make a little money today. Remind him that it was his loss when you walked out—not yours—and blame it on the manager.

Incidentally, if the direct approach doesn't seem to work, you may decide to try negotiating. If so, tear up the old purchase order. Right in front of your salesperson's nose. And ask for a new one.

When the salesperson asks with amazement what the hell you are doing, simply say that your previous offer was rejected, so it doesn't exist anymore. It is history. Then say, "If I have to jump through hoops to make a deal, I want a better one."

When he gets the new order form, write a new offer on it. Drop big time. Drop a thousand dollars below your first offer. You don't want to begin negotiating with an offer that puts the house into profit.

The salesperson will be thinking, "Oh, man, this stupid manager just cost me seventy-five bucks."

NEGOTIATION: OFFER—COUNTEROFFER

Or, more accurately, counter—counter—counter—counter, till everybody's blue in the face.

Here's a game plan, a set of offers to make. Each one is set at a point that has a particular relationship to cost.

The outline should help you to (a) know where you are and where you are going; (b) see where the house offer is in relation to yours; (c) show you where to stop and dig in your heels; (d) maintain your self-confidence by providing boundaries and road signs within the range of possible offers.

Write out something like the following, using the appropriate numbers, before going out to do the deal. But don't consider it written in stone. Negotiation is an ever-changing action-reaction process.

Checkpoints: Where to Place Your Offers

1. Way under, say 10% under cost (without pack).
Use this if the house starts high and seems reluctant to deal.
1a. The stall
Fiddle around, dance for a while. Use the "If I could, would you" routine. "What if I paid another sixty-five cents [or whatever] a month, that's thirty dollars more—would you lease me the car?" See what the salesperson says. Gauge her reaction. Will she start to deal? Or will she try to stonewall you, looking to gross big?

2. The ball price: cost minus freight, or cost without freight.
This is written down on the purchase order, signed, and backed with a deposit. You are not playing. This is not a talking point. You believe you can lease the car for this price, because someone has told you so. You have the saleswoman take this offer to her manager: cost without freight and the lease payment based on that price.

2a. Cost plus some of the freight.
But only after much confusion and complaint. Why wasn't your previous offer good enough? Why are they asking for more? Play it as it lays here. If the house offers small decreases in price, you offer tiny increases. As many tiny increases as it takes to bring them to their senses.

3. Invoice cost, that is, with freight but without pack.
3a. Cost plus a little.
And 3b, c, d, etc., if necessary. By "a little" I mean $25 to $40. You should have room for a number of offers before

reaching "dealer cost" because the pack will be at least $100 to $150.

4. *Cost plus pack, or dealer cost.*

But only after a lot of kicking and screaming. Figure $100 for pack on an inexpensive car, $150 on anything else. And when you reach this point ask about the pack. Is there one? How much? A salesman at another store said there was no pack at his store, why is there one here?

5. *Cost plus pack plus a little profit.*

$40 to $100 depending on the cost of the car. The deal you want should be in sight before you put the store into profit.

5a. *A lot of nickle-dime haggling (if needed) to bring them down to—or under—the price you want.*

Be prepared to be flexible. Modify the series of increases according to circumstances. If, for example, the store drops $20, then $32, then $16, you come up similar amounts. Piddling little price reductions deserve piddling little price increases. On the other hand, if the store drops big time, you can come up faster. But not too fast. Keep your increases smaller than their decreases, and keep the store's offers closer than yours to the price you will accept.

Moves and Countermoves

Let's turn now to some of the moves salespeople will make in the negotiation, the strategies behind them and your countermoves. I can't cover them all, but I can familiarize you with the basics. And negotiations usually repeat a small number of basic themes with a large number of variations, the variations being different justifications of the parties' points of view. Let's begin with an emergency measure you can use at any time with any approach—direct, negotiated, or by carrier pigeon.

Delaying Tactics: Slamming on the Brakes Suppose the salesperson's so slick that she tweaks your lust for the car and at the same time confuses you, filling you with self-doubt. You need to slow things down or bring them to a halt till you can regain your bearings. Here are two tactics that can be drawn out for as long as necessary.

1. Tell the salesperson that her payment seems wrong; it seems too high for her price. Then ask her to show you each step in her calculations.

2. Tell her you feel sudden, serious doubts about leasing. Then ask to see the lease contract. Then start reading it. Ask about this clause or that clause. Since it would take a day or so to read and understand the average lease contract, this should give you plenty of time to get yourself together.

Next, an answer to a common question no one asks aloud: *"What Do They Talk About When the Salesperson Goes Away?"*

They talk about you. The salesperson tells the manager what you said and what she said. The manager then asks questions about you: how much money you make, what you drive now, why you are getting a new car, etc. He's trying to figure you out, trying to decide what to do in order to get more money out of you. If he thinks of something, he suggests it to the salesperson. And, frequently, he criticizes any mistakes the salesperson was foolish enough to admit.

The salesperson will describe you and answer questions in a way designed to guide the manager into doing whatever she thinks is best. This is why you tell her you're sold on the car, you're sold on the store, and you want to do the deal right now.

- The closer she feels to her commission, the harder she'll try to persuade the manager to accept your deal.
- Your readiness to deal is almost as important to the manager as to the salesperson: Money now is both more certain and more valuable than money later. Your readiness to do the deal will increase the manager's willingness to accept the deal you want to do.

So, at least to begin with, use the carrot more than the stick. You will gain more control over salespeople by saying you want to make a deal than by threatening to deal somewhere else. You can always make the threat later. But before that, heighten the salesperson's desire for the deal, just as she heightens your desire for the car. Make her smell the money; make her feel she's only a fraction of an inch away from earning her commission.

To Get Things Rolling Unfortunately, you may have to make the threat early on.

The salesperson may write nothing more than a lease payment on the purchase order form. Suppose it's based on sticker price or sticker plus, but that information doesn't appear.

You ask that the price and acquisition cost be written on the order form. She answers that there is no price; leasing doesn't work that way. It's time for a small threat. Look sad, stand up, and shuffle toward the door.

She'll ask what the trouble is. Tell her you can't do business if the two of you are going to waste time trying to kid each other. There is a price and you both know it. After that, she'll either write a price on the order form or go to the manager to find out what to do, and then write down a price—which may or may not be accurate.

If the price is high, complain. Then make an offer at 10% under cost (invoice cost or cost before pack).

The saleswoman will be flabbergasted, insulted, indignant, stern, or all of the above, and ask you to justify your offer.

You can't. So what you do is dance. Ask what's wrong with your offer. Ask why her offer is so high. And do the old "If I could [pay another fifty, sixty cents a month] would you [lease me the car?]" shuffle. You are marking time. They have said nothing meaningful; you are not responding.

The salesperson will grow weary of the dance and deny that you believe what you are saying. She'll tell you she knows you don't really believe you can lease a car like this for that kind of money. Then she'll ask what it would take to lease you the car. Just give her a reasonable figure and she'll do her absolute best to get you the deal.

Now make your first serious offer. Tell her you've been shopping and someone at another dealership or lease store has offered you the car for the ball price (and acquisition cost, if different) of invoice cost minus freight.

Her move: "If it was such a good deal, why didn't you take it?" She's accusing you of telling a fib.

Tell her that this store is more convenient, or has such a reputation for honesty, good deals, and good service that you'd rather do the deal here. Use flattery whenever possible. They cannot disagree.

But be serious. Don't flatter facetiously or lightheartedly. This is a serious offer. You believe you can lease the car for this price. You want this offer written. Have the salesperson write it on the purchase order form: the price/acquisition cost and payment based on that price. Sign it. This is not a talking point, this is serious. Give her the deposit. And force her to take the offer to her manager.

She won't want to take it anywhere. It's way too low: The manager will make smartass remarks about her lack of ability. If she seems worried or a little fearful, provide her with an excuse to give to the manager. Tell her again that you've been shopping. You were told you could lease the car for this price and payment. Then sit tight.

Instead of seeming fearful, she may seem dead sure of herself and mount a heavy attack on the offer, telling you in ten different ways that it is obviously, ridiculously too low.

Don't waver. Say that you were quoted that price. But maybe she's right. Can she prove it? Then ask to see the invoice: the *whole* invoice, including the cost figures, not the retail figures.

Don't say this belligerently. You do not want to threaten or antagonize her, you want to give her the means to threaten her manager. The way to do that is to convince her that you're a heck of a nice person, but just about impossible to deal with. When she explains that to her manager, he will start changing his idea about how much profit he's going to make from you.

Now, your salesperson is in a bind. She does not want to take your offer to the manager. And even less does she want to ask the manager if she can show you the invoice.

But since you have convinced her that she must do one or the other, she'll take your deposit to the cashier and your offer to the manager. For the first and second commandments of a salesperson's job are to draw a signed offer from the customer, no matter how ridiculous, and to get that offer backed by a deposit.

If a salesperson refuses to accept a signed offer and deposit, the shit will hit the fan. Then it will hit the salesperson. If it happens more than a few times, she'll be fired. Avoiding splatter and keeping the job are powerful motivations. So no matter how many times she tells you that your offer is too low, too absurdly, embarrassingly low to show to her boss, sit tight, repeat your demand, and she will do it.

NOTE: Remember this basic move. When your salesperson throws up powerful resistance to your wishes, give her the alternatives of (a) taking to the manager an offer or a demand that will displease him or (b) showing you the cost figures on the invoice. And, at the same time, provide her with an excuse with which to protect herself from the manager's anger.

The Manager's Reaction to Your Offer at the Ball Price In a competitive market for vehicles in good supply, most managers are quick to spot a ball price. And most of the time they handle it in a relatively straightforward fashion. Believing that someone has promised you an impossible price, the manager will feel that his hands are pretty much tied. He'll figure his best bet is to explain to you that you've been offered a price below dealer cost, then offer you a very reasonable deal at a very small profit.

He will think this way because even a bargain price will be far higher than the ball price: freight plus pack plus profit. Thus, to make a profit of $200 on even a low-priced car like an Escort, you'll have to pay at least $600 more than you (supposedly) believe you have to pay. That's a lot of money. And a nice profit—$400 to $1,500—is a lot more. So the manager will feel that it's not safe to try for a decent profit. He fears that if he does, you'll leave. And probably not come back.

He believes that you will not come back *even after you find out that the other price was a fake.* Both research statistics and his own painful experience have pounded that belief into him. "Bebacks," people who walk out the door saying "I'll be back," very rarely come back. No matter why they leave, no matter why they say they'll be back.

So the manager may even send the salesman back with the invoice, willing to try anything to convince you that the ball price is fraudulent and his reasonable price, some $600 to $800 more, is honest.

This reasonable price should be very close to what you want—and maybe even better. It would not be unheard-of to make a deal at $285 over dealer cost on a $12,000 to $13,000 car, whereas you had been willing to pay up to, say, $350 over.

If this strategy works, you have your deal. And in a competitive market, there's a good chance it will work. If you are not in a competitive market, you may have to negotiate like the original Bargainer From Hell, or you may have to shop till you drop.

If the Strategy Doesn't Work

- The manager will make a counteroffer, either high or reasonable, with about half the markup chopped off.
- Or he will make no counter. There will be none written on the order form and the salesperson will not mention one.

In this case, the manager will tell the salesperson that you are so far away (your offer is so low) that it makes no sense for her to commit the house yet. He will instruct the salesperson to draw a higher offer out of you before he (the manager) offers a lower price.

"Commit the house" means stand by the offer. Normally, a manager's offer equals the house offer equals the deal you get if you accept. And normally, when the salesperson says that the manager offered such and such, she is quoting, and the offer is for real. If you accept it, you have the deal. But when a salesperson says, "What if I could lease you the car for X dollars," and you accept, it means nothing until the manager accepts your acceptance.

If the manager makes no counter, the salesperson will say something like: "Look, we're just not in the right ballpark here. We have to get realistic. A car like this is worth a lot more than you're offering."

Your Task: Obtain a Counteroffer from the Manager The house should come down before you come up. Come down in concrete terms, not in terms of the salesperson's "If I could, would you?" Tell the salesperson you want a counteroffer from the manager.

If he answers by talking about wrong ballparks and such, ignore him. Don't waste your energy. Think about the beach again. Be silent.

The enormous pressure of your silence will work quickly. He'll ask what's wrong.

Tell him again that you need a counteroffer. You can't do anything till you get a counteroffer.

He'll say, "Well, what if I could lease you the car for—"

You say, "No, not what if you could do this or that. An offer from the manager." Tell him that you really want to do business with him. But, since you know they have some kind of discount in mind to start with, you need to know what it is. You have to know where you're starting from. Otherwise, you're dead in the water.

This gives him an explanation for the manager. It blames the manager; it deflects the burden of incompetence the manager will try to lay on him. Remember, if a manager suspects that you are refusing to pay more because the salesperson is not doing his job properly, he will probably not lower his price.

This time, when the salesman goes away, he'll come back

with a counter. As before, it may be high (a hundred or two off), it may be reasonable (about half the markup lopped off), or it may be low (right around where you want to be). If the last, you have a done deal. With the others, you respond as before, except that now, since you are not cutting the process short, your responses are more elaborate.

Let's assume the counter is high (about $100 off on an Escort, $300 off on a car marked up $2,000). And it's your move.

Your objectives:

- To force them to explain cost to you, then offer you a super deal. Failing that:
- To squeeze them into chopping off 50% of the markup (with corresponding reduction in lease payment) before you start the real work of haggling.

If the manager counters high, act as if he had made no counter at all. Refuse to move. Make no offer. You and the manager are so far apart that it makes no sense for you to come up till he comes down. Do the following:

- Complain. Tell the salesperson you can't understand what's going on. You thought you could get a good deal here. But the manager didn't take anything off!

  They'll tell you it is a good deal. The only reason you don't think so is that your idea of the price is far too low, completely unrealistic.
- Ask why it's too low. After all, someone told you they would lease the car for that price. Were they lying? How do you know whom to believe?
- Deliver the punchline: Ask to see the invoice, so you can find out for yourself whom to believe.

  If the salesperson tries to avoid this issue, insist on it. Lead him to mention the word "cost." If he doesn't say it on his own, make him say it by asking again why your price is too low. Is it below cost?

The more your salesperson discusses cost and the invoice, the more logical and inevitable your good deal comes to seem. And the more logical and inevitable he makes it appear to the manager.

- If the salesperson seems too inexperienced to know what cost is, tell him to find out from the manager. Tell him you have a problem with these wildly differing prices from different dealers and you need to find out what's going on.
- Some car store managers are nasty. They turn especially nasty when told a customer wants to see an invoice. If your salesperson seems to be worried, a little fearful, when asked for the invoice, give him an excuse. Example: "Look, blame it on me. Tell him I'm a no-good, cheap, chiseling, nickle-dime blankety-blank. So we're not going to get anywhere here until I find out what's going on."
- If the salesperson seems a little nasty himself, if he keeps belittling your offer, or if he tries to act tough, stonewalling you or bullying you, bully him back. Tell him that the high counteroffer is so far over the other dealers' (or lease store) prices that it's insulting. Is he going to explain why it's so high, or just keep insulting you? And if he's not willing to explain, maybe he should give back your deposit.

Give back? This is like a brush with death.

So he'll go see the manager and report what you've said. He'll describe the difficulty he's having with you, emphasizing and exaggerating how close you were to walking out the door. He'll do everything he can to sell the manager the idea that you have to get a good deal. And now, as long as the manager has a halfway decent opinion of the salesperson's abilities, the manager will either respond to the ball, and you'll have your deal, or will be reasonable, and you'll say goodbye to 50% or more of the markup.

After losing half the markup on an inexpensive car like an Escort, you need only to negotiate away another hundred or two to have a great deal. But on a car marked up a thousand or more, you still have quite a way to go.

HAGGLING

Look disappointed. Complain. Work the deal. Do some horse-trading. Make a series of verbal offers, coming up in small increments, always trying to draw lower offers from the salesperson. Use the tried and true "If I could, would you?" "What if I could come up with another twenty dollars? What would that be, fifty cents a month? Could we do business?"

If she says no, come up, maybe, $45 on the price. And say that "forty-five" as if it were "forty-five thousand."

After your offer has grown to, say, $50 to $75 more than the first, have it written, sign it and force her to take it to the manager. If necessary, grow somewhat indignant. Tell her you keep offering more and more and she keeps saying no. Well, you're unhappy. She'd better do everything she can to get you this one. No matter how much she protests that you're not being realistic, or you're way off base, or you're playing football with a hockey puck, or whatever. You have been offering more and more. What does she want, blood? She'd better give this one a shot for you, her best shot.

She'll go up to the boss and come back with a lower offer.

In this fashion, back and forth—making tiny verbal increases, then writing and signing the offer every time it reaches $40 to $75 dollars beyond the previous one—work your way up. Don't worry about how many times the salesperson goes back and forth between you and the manager. I've done it seven or eight times and have seen others do it as many as twelve times. You have plenty of time—make sure you have plenty of time—and you have plenty of room. Assuming freight is $300 to $500 and the house pack is $150, you have $450 to $650 worth of room before you get to dealer cost. If you are coming up $40 to

$75 each time you make a signed offer, you can make quite a few of them before you arrive anywhere serious.

Time after time, the salesperson will carry your offer to the boss—yet still be unable to put the house into profit. At some point, the manager should admit that you know what you want and are determined to have it. Then he'll get off his price and make a serious move toward yours.

House Tactics If the Manager Turns Stubborn

The Bluff

At some point while the house offer is still high, the manager may decide to beat the drums and fire the guns and see if he can scare you into taking his deal.

This will be like the medium counter in the direct approach—only it will be all out. The manager will stand on his previous offer and tell the salesperson to hammer you. Very possibly, he'll bluff the salesperson, too, telling her to get the price or lose the deal.

Then, to you, she will insist, over and over, that they are down to the bone; there is no more markup left to take off; they can go no lower. Nobody can. Nobody can beat the deal they're offering. She will speak with the voice of authority; if she's any good, she will sound like she's telling the truth.

Next, she may employ pressure tactics: tell you that the factory raised the price of the car; try to wear you down; show you spurious documents, downgrade your trade with a vengeance (if you have one), and try to humiliate you by saying maybe you are looking at too much car, maybe you should switch to a less expensive one—or maybe you should think about a used car.

You know what to do.

Point out that what she's saying may be true, but if she wants your business, she will have to prove it. Proof is the invoice, the cost part of the invoice.

Resistance to Showing the Invoice

- The salesperson may ask you what business you're in. Suppose you are in water heaters. She'll ask, "If I bought a water heater from you, would you show me the invoice?"

  You say: "No, I wouldn't. But this is the car business."

  That line will explain almost anything you want it to. It means simply that since cars are the only store-bought item you bargain over, everything is different. As, in fact, it is.
- She may tell you that she really wants to show you the invoice. But she's not allowed to: Store policy forbids it.

  Say: "But your manager can do it anyway. So go tell your manager I need to see it."
- She may say that even the manager isn't allowed to show invoices. The owner won't let him.

  Say: "Well, you'd better give the owner a call. Or you'd better give back my deposit."

What Will It Take?

Again, the salesperson will say that they cannot meet your price. But instead of hammering you, she'll plead with you, saying if they *could* meet your price, they'd do it in a minute. After all, they're here to sell cars. Doesn't that make sense? Of course it does. So just give her any reasonable offer and she'll walk through fire to get it for you.

The point here is not to hammer you into taking their deal, but to persuade you to raise your offer more than you have been. You've been coming up $24, $40, $55 a pop. Now, she's trying to lure you into raising your offer by a few hundred.

- Don't do it. Toss the ball back into her court. Ask her for a reasonable offer. If it's not reasonable enough, say so. Tell her

that by "reasonable," you mean the best she can do: the best deal she ever gave anybody. Make her work. Make her sweat. Make her feel that you are getting ready to walk.
- Bring up the pack. Mention a lease store and say that the lease store didn't have a pack. Then ask how much her pack is. Press hard for an answer.

   She answers. Okay, you accept the pack. So, considering the pack, what's the best she can do? Does she really want to make you go somewhere else? Even though you'd rather do business with her?
- If she dodges your questions, offer ten dollars more on the price. She'll complain, say it's impossible. Ask why she wanted to know what it would take if she doesn't want to do it.

Temptation: The Salesperson Offers a Price You Like

At some point, perhaps in exasperation, perhaps after you ask her for the best she can do, the salesperson may make an offer at a great price. Maybe $100 to $200 over dealer cost (a "hundred-dollar deal," a "deuce deal"). A super deal—that gets you into profit so the salesperson can save face.

Should you sign at that price? No.

Suppose you have worked your way up to somewhere around invoice cost. A hundred-dollar deal will be $100 plus pack ($150) more, or $250 over your current offer. You have not been coming up in big jumps like that and you don't want to start now. For if the manager refuses the deal, as he will, you are suddenly $250 ahead of your game plan. You have been whip-sawed, sucked into offering more than you planned, only to be refused.

How to Handle Temptation

Demand a preapproved offer. Tell the salesperson her offer sounds good. But you are getting sick and tired of making offers and having them rejected. You've had it.

Therefore, tell her to go ask the manager if he will take the price she just mentioned. If the boss says yes, you'll sign. Otherwise, no. You are not signing any more offers just to have them thrown back in your face.

If the manager has a nasty streak, it will show in glorious technicolor when she asks him to approve a price you haven't signed for. So she'll give you a hundred reasons why she can't do it.

Again, tell her to blame you. You are a no-good, chiseling so-and-so. Nevertheless, you are the customer and the customer is always right. Don't be bashful about saying that. It will remind her that she has to *earn* your goodwill and your business.

She'll go. The manager will say yes or no. If no, and the store is a dealing store, the counter will be a deal price. And you'll have what you want.

What If Nothing Works?

I've seen all these tactics work successfully. But sometimes nothing works. The negotiation goes into gridlock. There's a logjam in the deal. You make . . .

. . . Your Last Offer

Offer a small profit, maybe $50 over dealer cost (cost with pack). Then say, "This is it. Bring me the deal or bring back my deposit."

The manager may refuse the deal, but he won't give your money back. Instead, he'll make yet another counteroffer. If he drops to something close to the deal you want, forget what you've just said. The logjam is gone. Haggling has started to work. So return to it: Offer another few dollars on the price.

And if the counter comes back too high?

Well, *now* you remember what you said. Tell the salesperson to go get your deposit. Don't be angry. Be sad. All this time and effort and you still can't make a deal. Too bad.

Rather than dashing off to get your money, the salesperson will probably ask you for a "little help." Just another $200. Next to nothing. Five dollars a month. A dollar a week. Pennies. The improved gas mileage or increased reliability of the new car will save you five times that.

Don't fall for the "just-a-little-help-it's-only-pennies" line. Send the salesperson back to get your deposit.

Instead of your deposit, you should now get your deal. Or get it after making one more offer.

Or—this is unlikely but it could happen—the manager will stand pat. Then you will demand your money back and leave.

Or the store may try its knockout punch.

The T.O., or Turnover

They don't turn you over and shake till your money falls out; they turn you over to another person.

After the salesperson fails a number of times to raise you, either a closer (a specialist in making deals with difficult customers) or a manager comes in. It's someone new, a fresh face, someone full of energy, ready to work you over, ready to tell you that you can't buy steak for the price of baloney.

Don't be intimidated. And if it's a manager, don't feel flattered to be dealing with a honcho.

Simply follow the script laid out above, starting from wherever you are in the deal. Be sure to (a) say that you thought this store gave good deals and (b) blame the manager. Blame the manager for all previous failures to make the deal. Say that you like the place and you like Rodney or Sally Salespro and you really want to do business with them. But you are not going to do business if he (the manager) won't let them give you a half-decent deal.

The manager may respond by getting tough. In a stern, nononsense voice, he will—well, basically, he'll simply repeat the salesperson's moves. But the message will be "I know what I'm talking about. I'm the boss."

No matter how bosslike and tough the manager is, even if he's a lot tougher than you, don't waver. Do what you did before: Remind him (and perhaps yourself) that he needs you more than you need him; make him justify whatever he says; and lead him to cost and the invoice.

I'll tell you a secret about T.O.'s. Once a manager hoists himself off his seat, rarely will he let you go without making a deal. He'll spend a decade or two trying to force the salesperson to get, say, $500 profit on a $12,000 car. The salesperson fails and fails. The manager makes him feel like a piece of human garbage. Then the manager takes control. He swings his shoulders around and swaggers into the salesperson's office. This is a big-time honcho you're dealing with here. He's tough as nails. There's no way you're getting away from this guy. And then he closes you.

At $300 over.

A DEAL WITH A TRADE

When you trade in, the deal is a little more complicated. Assuming that you use your trade equity as a downstroke, there will be a couple more numbers for you to consider—and therefore a couple more ways for you to be hoodwinked.

If you put the trade equity down on the lease, then sell price minus trade allowance equals cash difference.

If you owe nothing on the trade and put nothing else down, then the cash difference will equal the acquisition cost for the leased car. If, however, you owe money on the trade, you must add back the lien payoff. Then the acquisition cost equals the cash difference plus the amount needed to pay off the lien.

Let's suppose you have looked up the value of your car in the current wholesale price book that your local dealers use. You've followed directions carefully and determined that wholesale on the car is $1,550.

Then you went out and shopped it at four used-car stores. You were offered $1,500, $1,525, and $1,550 twice.

The new car, a Chevy Caprice Wagon, is the base model but not too badly equipped. It has a sticker price of $14,820.

We'll assume that there are no package discounts on the Caprice, that its residual value is 32%, and that the lease will run 48 months at 10% with no bank fee. Assume you look up cost in your cost and price book and find that invoice cost, including freight, advertising, and finance charges is $12,855.

Further assume that your cost book shows the freight charge to be $480. Subtracting that from the invoice cost ($12,855 − $480) gives us a cost without freight of $12,375.

Then adding $150 to invioice cost for the pack ($12,855 + $150) gives us a dealer cost of $13,005.

Now we have three costs:

Cost without Freight	$12,375
Invoice cost	$12,855
Dealer cost	$13,005

After $13,005 we are in profit. Adding amounts to dealer cost gives us a price based on a certain amount of profit. For example:

Dealer cost	$13,005
+ $100 profit	$13,105
+ $200 profit	$13,205
+ $295 profit	$13,300
And so on, up to sticker price	$14,820

Let's say you're willing to pay $385 over dealer cost. Your deal would look like this:

Dealer Cost + Profit = Price − Wholesale Price on Trade = Cash Difference
$13,005 + $385 = $13,390 − $1,550 = $11,840

STORE POLICY: WORK FROM STICKER PRICE DOWN— NOT FROM COST UP

As you can see, selling price minus the wholesale value or cash value of your trade equals the cash difference. And reversing the operation shows that the price you pay is the cash difference plus the wholesale value of your trade.

No one in the store, however, will want to discuss this little fact with you. They will try to deal from retail or sticker price. If the deal is settled at a cash difference of $11,840, they will try to show you the deal this way:

$$\text{Price} - \text{Trade Allowance} = \text{Cash Difference}$$
$$\$14,820 - \$2,980 = \$11,840$$

What is a trade allowance? It is the cash value of the trade-in (hard dollars) plus the amount discounted off the sticker price of the new car (show dollars).

No one will want to discuss these distinctions with you because managers and salespeople have learned that working from sticker and showing discounts as increased trade allowances is more effective, both in satisfying customers and in getting big grosses. Notice that "both." People will sometimes pay more so they can believe they got more for their car.

To determine the cash difference, then, the store will not subtract wholesale from a discounted price; it will subtract trade allowance (wholesale plus discount) from the retail price.

WORKING FROM COST UP TO ESTABLISH CASH DIFFERENCE

In the example, our trade equity is serving as a down payment. We are putting no other money down and we owe nothing on the trade. Therefore, the cash difference will equal the lease acquisition cost.

Now, if you were going out to lease the Caprice, all you would really have to do is the set of numbers at the highest amount you are willing to pay, or $385 over dealer cost.

But that is not what you should do. The more familiar you are with the entire range of possible numbers on the vehicles in question, the less likely you are to be victimized.

You should prepare something like this: a list of costs, profits, sell prices, cash differences (price minus wholesale value), lease payments based on those cash differences, and trade allowances. The list should range from the lowest offer you are likely to make to the highest price they are likely to ask.

	Cost/Sell Price	Whole-sale on Trade	Cash Difference	Lease Payment	Trade Allowance
$1200 under invoice cost	$11,655 −	$1,550 =	$10,105	$173.59	$4,715
Cost less freight	$12,375 −	1,550 =	10,825	191.60	3,995
Invoice cost	$12,855 −	1,550 =	11,305	203.60	3,515
Cost + 150 pack or Dealer cost	$13,005 −	1,550 =	11,455	207.34	3,365
When we add profit cost becomes	Price				
Dealer cost + $100	$13,105 −	1,550 =	11,555	209.84	3,265
+ $200 profit	$13,205 −	1,550 =	11,655	212.34	3,165
+ $300 profit	$13,305 −	1,550 =	11,755	214.84	3,065
+ $385 profit	$13,390 −	1,550 =	11,840	216.97	2,980
+ $400 profit	$13,405 −	1,550 =	11,855	217.34	2,965
Sticker price	$14,820 −	1,550 =	13,270	252.72	1,550
$800 over sticker	$15,620 −	1,550 =	14,070	272.72	1,550
Same $800 over	$14,820 −	750 =	14,070	272.72	750

In the last two items, notice that it doesn't matter whether the price of the car goes up or the amount paid for the trade goes down. Also note: "trade allowances" are obtained by subtracting the cash difference from the sticker price of $14,820. If making a list like this seems to be a lot of work, bear in mind that the more familiar you are with the entire range of numbers, the better you will understand every aspect of your deal and every offer your salesperson makes. (Incidentally, a fringe benefit of doing a list like this is that it enables you to see the difference that adding or subtracting $100 from the price makes in the lease payment.)

If You Hate Numbers

If you have a mental block against numbers, can only handle one or two at a time, and therefore must think in terms of sticker price minus trade allowance, do this:

Figure out the effective (after pack) markup on the car: Sticker price of $14,820 minus dealer cost (including pack) of $13,005 equals an effective markup of $1,815.

From that, subtract the amount of profit you are willing to pay. $1,815 − $385 = $1,430.

Now add the discount of $1,430 to the cash value of your car. $1,430 + $1,550 = $2,980 trade allowance. Take sticker price, $14,820 − $2,980 and you have the cash difference of $11,840.

The first way is a bit more complicated, but better. Too many people worry about what they are getting "off." But the size of the discount is irrelevant. After all, dealers add protection packages and decor groups so they can show huge discounts while sacrificing very little profit. Profit is what counts: the amount over cost. Make the effort to list all the costs, profits, cash differences, and so on. Worry about the amount the dealer is putting on, not the amount you are getting off.

AT THE STORE

When you have a trade-in, there are two ways to talk about the deal:

1. You can force the conversation to focus on wholesale numbers: discounted price minus the actual cash value of the trade-in.

2. Or talk in the store's own terms: sticker price minus the trade allowance.

If you go with the direct approach rather than negotiate, it probably makes no difference which one of these you choose.

If you negotiate, the way you talk about the value of your trade-in may influence the way the salesperson perceives you.

Talk about the wholesale or actual cash value of your car and your salesperson may well figure you for a smart guy who did his or her homework.

The advantage is that they may then decide that they have no chance to score off you and try to get you your deal as quickly as possible. Then again, your salesperson may not have enough experience to know what you're talking about.

A potential disadvantage is that the salesperson may not believe you've been balled if you make an offer at cost minus freight. If you want to try that tactic and still use wholesale numbers, spell out those numbers. Say that you talked to someone who told you they would lease you the car for $12,375 (invoice cost without freight) less $1,550 for your car. That's what they said your car was worth. Then you took it to a used-car dealer and he said the same thing.

To make an offer at the ball price using retail numbers, simply say you were offered $3,995 for the trade.

Which should you choose, dealer cost plus profit (which adds up to a discounted price) minus wholesale value for your car—or sticker price minus trade allowance? The answer has to be the one you are more comfortable with. Do make an effort, however, to become comfortable working with cost plus profit minus wholesale value. The numbers are more precise; there are fewer chances for mistakes.

DEALING—THE SAME WITH A FEW DIFFERENCES: HOW THE STORE WILL HANDLE YOUR CAR

The salesperson will look over your car then describe it to his manager. Normally, the manager will tell him to start the deal by offering you considerably less than the car's wholesale value. With our hypothetical car, worth around $1,550, the first offer would probably be $700 to $900.

Turn back for a second to the list of cost, prices, etc., and look at the first and last items.

The last item is labeled "$800 over sticker." Whether the price of the new car goes up, or the amount paid for your car goes down, the result is the same $272 lease payment.

If you encounter this kind of offer, hit back with the $173 payment that begins the list. This should inform the salesperson immediately that they will not be able to jerk you around: It will begin the process of their education.

With or without a trade-in, the salesperson will probably try to avoid mentioning any numbers besides the lease payment.

Instead, as Lorna did, he will inform you of the cost of buying: $385 a month on a 48-month loan. (Giving you $750 for your trade-in, charging you 11%: both unstated.)

Then, like Skinny Tie (who claimed not to know any numbers at all), he'll tell you leasing will save you a whole lot of money. And then, with a note of urgency, tell you that on a 48-month lease, "I can put you in that car right now for two-ninety a month. Tax included. No money down. Save you ninety-five dollars a month."

The buy payment quote is for a deal at $800 over sticker, with an extra half percent tacked on the interest rate. This is to make the lease payment look better, even though it, too, is $800 over sticker.

THE PURCHASE ORDER FORM WITH A TRADE-IN

Before demanding all the figures in writing on the order form, do a little preliminary wrestling over your trade. Ask how much you are getting for your car.

Since the salesperson has made an outrageous offer, he'll probably be vague, saying that he thinks the boss figured over $2,000. Probably around $2,400.

Returning to your lowest figures ($1,200 under cost in this example), say you expected around $4,600 for yours. And to lease the wagon for about $175 a month.

As before, he'll ask where in the world you got your numbers. Tell him you've seen cars like yours on dealers' lots for about that. Maybe you're asking a little too much, but it doesn't seem that far off. Why won't he give you that much? (Ask him to justify his refusal and his numbers rather than bothering much about justifying yours.)

He'll tell you he sells cars like yours every day for $2,600, so what are you talking about? But what if—and now he will become intense: "What if I could lease you that car right now for $285 a month? Plus your trade. Maybe even a hair under. That would save you *a hundred dollars* a month. On a full-sized wagon with a 305-cubic-inch V-8 motor—that's a super payment for a car like that. So just give me your okay right down here and let me see if I can talk the boss into it for you."

Having reduced his price (by about $200), he'll go for the close. He'll write that offer on the purchase order and turn it around to face you, ready for your signature. He will shut up and stare at you.

At this point don't bother asking for a bigger discount, or making another offer, or justifying your price. Instead, begin your demand for all the figures in writing. Start by tearing apart his price. On the purchase order he will have written something like "Customer will lease for 48 months at $285 a month, tax included, plus trade."

As before, the purchase order should lay out all the terms of the deal. Something like the following:

Retail price	$14,820.00
Trade allowance	− 900.00
Cash difference	$13,920.00
48-month lease payment based on	
acquisition cost of $13,920	268.97
6% tax	+ 16.14
Lease payment with tax	$ 285.11

You can see why it won't say this. Demand that it does.

Write on it "Retail price: $14,820."

Then write "trade" and ask what you are being paid for your car.

He may head for the manager's desk to find out what to say. He may repeat his earlier vagueness: "Oh, around twenty-four hundred." He may pull a higher number out of the air, trying for something he figures will make you happy. Assume that he says $2,600. Whatever it is, write it on the purchase order.

Retail price	$14,820
Trade allowance	− 2,600
Cash difference	$12,220

Then write, "48-month lease payment based on $12,220." and ask, "You figured your two-eighty-five payment on a price of twelve-two?" Then shut up and stare at him.

If he didn't realize he had a problem before, he'll realize it now. He is on the verge of committing himself in writing to a lie. This is a no-no.

He will try various ways of evading your questions. Be patient for a little while; he has to do this, it's his job. But after that little while goes by, point out to him that he should answer questions you are completely entitled to ask.

Now he's stuck. He will probably go see the manager to find

out what to tell you. And to escape for a while, giving you time to forget, he hopes, what you just asked him.

When he comes back, he may admit making a mistake or he may try to be stern and to bully you, as before, telling you that you know as well as he does that your car's not worth $4,600. So if you are serious, you'd better get realistic. And then, of course, he'll do his absolute best to get you any kind of realistic or reasonable figure.

Now go with whatever you have chosen: the direct approach or the negotiation. And things will be pretty much as before—except there are more items to have written down on the purchase order.

These extra items may create an extra problem with the manager. He may ignore your requests and persist in countering your offers with: "Dear Ms. [or Mr.] Jones, we need $251.17 [or whatever] a month for forty-eight months plus tax and trade."

Tell the salesperson to inform him that you have to have everything written on the order form. Dangle the carrot; show the stick. The place has a good reputation and you really want to do the deal here—but if they refuse to write everything down, you'll have to go somewhere else.

And be willing to do it; be willing to actually walk out.

Typical Dodges

- The salesperson may tell you not to worry about having things written down. Just wait till the Business Manager puts it on the computer, then you'll see everything. Refuse. You want it now, on the purchase order form.
- If he says they can't do it now, because they don't have the information till the computer figures it out, he's lying. Threaten to leave.

You are the customer; you are correct to request this information in writing and you are entitled to it. So go after it. Accept no excuses, and you'll get it.

SEVEN

Keep On
Keeping On

NEGOTIATING THE END-OF-TERM BUYOUT

When the lease expires, the end-of-term buyout (or payoff, or purchase price) is the amount you must pay if you want to buy, sell, or trade the car. You must clear your debt to sell or trade in, so this amount determines whether or not you have equity in the car and can make any money on it.

In many instances, the lease-end buyout is negotiable. But you have to discover for yourself if your deal is one of those instances. And as time goes on, this negotiation may become more difficult. Many lenders are discovering (during 1989) that two to five years ago they had overestimated the residual values of leased cars. Now, not getting what they thought they'd get for the cars, they feel they are losing money. Some of these companies will start to underestimate residuals, raise their monthly lease payments, and yet continue to overcharge you on the buyout. Many such companies will price themselves out of the business.

Others, however, will do what we have seen BankLease doing: structure the payment with one residual for themselves and another for you. Many of these companies will still offer good deals. And because of the size of spread between the two buyouts, many of them should be willing to negotiate the one for you.

The time to try negotiating is right after you reach agreement on price and payment. If you're tired and decide to go home, you may be stuck forever with the high residual written into the contract. Or, if you wait till a couple months before the lease expires, then call the lessor, you are likely to encounter a runaround.

The lessor will tell you to call your dealer or lease store. The store will tell you they have to check. Then they'll call the lessor—who will get the information from its computer in about a minute. And, finally, the store will call you back and quote a number, a number which will include a $400 to $500 markup.

Routinely, we inflated the balance owed on leased vehicles by $400 to $500. Almost every time, for almost every customer. And we were a respectable business: very similar in our practices to many other respectable businesses.

Why does this happen? By forcing you to contact the leasing dealer or lease store, the lessor rewards the place that wrote your lease with an opportunity to do some repeat business. That store now has a chance to lease you another car.

Or, if you buy out the lease, the store has an opportunity to sell a used car without risking any investment. The dealer handles your buyout as if it were just another sale. You pay the lessor's buyout plus the dealer's profit. As far as the lessor is concerned, the dealer's profit is his own business.

You cannot get around this cozy little arrangement by calling the lessor and pretending to be Sid Schmelp at Feebleman Ford. For when you ask for the buyout, the lessor will ask, in return, for your secret code number. They will not tell you the balance owed unless you tell them the secret number. It's like being in a spy movie.

And you can't get around the arrangement by paying your salesman a few bucks to find out for you. Nine times out of ten your salesperson won't have the code number, either. That number is a closely guarded secret. The dealer changes it periodically and does not tell the salespeople what it is. So the salesperson will have to ask a manager or the finance guy to call the lessor. Whoever makes the call will add the markup before telling the salesman.

When I moved to Pennsylvania, I called Ford Credit. Telling them I was Joe Paganelli, I asked for my lease buyout. They didn't even bother to find out if a guy named Paganelli had leased a car from them. They said, "We don't have that information. You'll have to call your dealer."

I said I wanted to talk to the manager and, when I got the manager, immediately began badgering her. I told her I owed the money to Ford and I didn't want to talk to any dealer. I wanted her to tell me what the balance was.

She repeated the same line. I kept on browbeating her, not shouting, but letting my voice rise, and finally she slipped up.

"The amount of the buyout is something you have to negotiate with the dealer," she said.

And hung up on me.

Ford Credit is by no means alone in this practice. Walking into a randomly chosen savings-and-loan, I said I wanted to speak to someone about my lease buyout. They said they were very sorry, but I'd have to talk to my dealer.

Obviously, when you talk to your dealer, you cannot negotiate if you don't know that there is a need to negotiate; don't even know that there is a negotiable amount involved. And in many cases no one will tell you. Many salespeople, in fact, can't tell you, because they don't know, either. They believe that the lease buyout is like the remaining balance on a loan, which, of course, is not negotiable. And they conclude that, therefore, neither is the remaining balance on a lease.

Why Can't You Tell That Something's Fishy?

Because the residual value will be so much higher than the actual buyout that, even after the dealer adds four or five on top, the amount quoted to you will be lower than you expected.

When this nice, low number comes over the phone, customers are pleasantly surprised. They think they're getting away with something . . . a couple of hundred somethings, in fact. So they keep their surprise to themselves and sort of wallow in happiness . . . even as they get burned.

What can you do about this? Negotiate, negotiate, negotiate. And it may not be easy.

If You Have Not Yet Leased the Car

Calculate an estimated buyout. This will be one of your last chores, for to do it you need to know what the terms of the deal will be. Then, determine the going rate on auto loans around town. If it's 10.5%, assume the lender will want at least a 10.5% return on its investment in the leased car.

Then, as we did before, figure out how much the lender has absolutely at risk. Potentially at risk is the price of the car plus the residual value. Absolutely at risk is the price of the car: the money paid to buy it. Let's return to the Escort for a number and say the lender has put out $8,000.

Assuming your lease runs 48 months, what would that money earn over four years at 10.5%?

Get the four-year 10.5% factor from a loan payment chart. It's .02561. Multiply $8,000 by .02561. The answer is $204.88. Multiply $204.88 by 48 (months): $9,834.24. That's the amount collected on $8,000 lent for four years at 10.5% interest.

Next, get the total of *your* lease payments. Using the Escort numbers for illustration, multiply $157.56 by 48: $7,562.88.

Subtract that from $9,834.24: a buyout of $2,271.36 would ensure a 10.5% return on the purchase price of $8,000.

Now you have an idea of what the lessor has to get in order for the investment to make sense at the going rate of interest. It's a great deal lower than the residual of $2,920, isn't it?

Next, if you have a financial calculator, do an amortization schedule for the lease. If you don't have one, call a bank. Tell them you are thinking about leasing and want to find out what the remaining balance would be on a lease with whatever your terms are. For our example here, the answer is $2,432.

Add $100 for the dealer or lease store: $2,532. Now you have a range: from $2,271 to $2,532.

What to Shoot For

Twenty-two seventy-one. Try to set a buyout that gives you the car at a total cost no higher than the total cost on a straight installment purchase at the going rate. Shoot for that, but be willing to settle for a hundred or two more. You should not weep and gnash your teeth if you end up with a buyout of, say, $2,500 to $2,600. In our no-free-lunch universe, you cannot reasonably expect to get the benefit of leasing's low payments for free. But you can try.

Exception

If you have searched out a deal with the highest possible residual actually used to figure the payment, resulting in the lowest payment possible, you can try to negotiate the buyout, but don't count on being successful. To illustrate, let's look at the Escort as if put through a bank just entering the leasing business and using extremely high residuals.

The acquisition cost would be $8,200. The residual: 39%, or $3,559. The rate: 10.8%. And the payment: $149.60 for 48 months. Here, the balance due, or end-of-term buyout, will be the residual value. And the bank will want to get it. But, as the high residual indicates, the bank also wants business, so it would be worthwhile to try for a better deal. Calculating the total of payments on a buy at 10.8%, then subtracting the total of payments on the lease (as we did in the preceding example) leaves a difference of $2,755. That would be your bargain buyout, the starting point for your negotiations. Any ending point below $3,559 would be a plus.

DOING IT

Prepare the buyout figures before going in to do the deal.

Then, during the deal, you can both test the waters to estimate your chances for success and at the same time set up the coming negotiation. Ask the salesperson, "What if I want to buy the car at the end of the lease? How will the cost compare to buying right from the start?"

Some stores, and some lenders, will tell you that leasing is designed to give you a low monthly payment, not to finance a buy. This will hint that the buyout will be hard to negotiate.

Others, however, will tell you that the total cost of leasing and buying at the end will be about the same as buying from the beginning. Or within a hundred dollars or so. And they may throw in, "And maybe even less."

If that's what you hear, repeat it and make sure they say it again. Ask if they're sure. Have them say it often enough so that they cannot forget that they said it.

Don't do anything more for the time being. Wait till you've reached an agreement on price. Then, just before signing the final time, say, "Wait a minute. What will the buyout be?"

Still using the Escort as an example, the salesperson will say, "Oh, twenty-eight, twenty-nine hundred, in around there."

Tell her, no, you think it should be in around twenty-two hundred.

When she asks where you got your figures, explain that buying the car for $8,000 at 10.5% for four years would be $204.88 a month, times the 48 months would be $9,834.

You, however, are paying $157.56 times 48, or about $7,600. About a $2,200 difference. So that's what your buyout should be, right? Didn't she say it would cost about the same to buy at the end of the lease as it would to buy in the first place? Isn't that around $2,200?

In Comes the Manager

Your salesperson will probably not know what to do next, so she'll go get a manager.

Repeat what you just said. If the manager asks for an explanation of your figures, give him the same one.

He will say, "Wrong."

Ask him to explain why.

He may not explain anything. Instead, he may say a couple of things that you should *not* settle for:

"Don't worry about it, you'll see it in the contract."

Or "We can't give it to you now; it has to be worked out on the computer. So just sign the deal and then we'll take you in to see the Business Manager and he'll explain everything."

Refuse these invitations. All it takes to figure it out is a pencil, a piece of paper, a five-dollar calculator, and a couple of minutes. Tell the manager that it has to be taken care of right now. You might mention that you've shopped at a dealer nearby who was willing to cut down the buyout.

But do not be in a hurry to leave. This is not like going down the street to Fred's Ford and beating a deal by $20. So make your threats mildly, here. But keep in mind that they want to move that unit and they want to move it now, to you. Which provides you with a big stick.

An Argument That May Give You Trouble

The manager may tell you that your low lease payment will not pay off all of the money the lessor pays for the car. Therefore, you owe interest on all that unreduced principal.

However, if you have an amortization schedule run, you'll find that you pay as much or more interest in actual dollars on a lease as you would on a buy. In other words, the interest paid on the Escort lease is about the same as the interest you'd pay if you borrowed money to buy it. What remains unpaid on the lease is principal. But, in a way, this is an accounting quibble.

So if the manager argues that you will owe interest on the unreduced principal, don't argue back. Instead, try to brush the whole point aside. Say, "Yeah, but I'll pay as much interest on the lease as on the buy, so it doesn't matter." This is true, but don't press the point. Change the subject.

There's a very good chance that the manager won't bring up this argument. He may, however, bring up an elaborate and specious argument—which could be based on anything at all— "proving" a buyout of $2,920. Remember, I "proved" to a customer that I leased him a truck for $7,000 when the real price was almost $10,000.

Again, avoid discussion. To answer either of these arguments, tell him that, however it works, the buyout can't be $2,920.

He will ask, in a slightly threatening way, "Whadda ya mean? Why not?"

You say, "Because Sally Salespro here told me that buying the car at the end of the lease would cost within a hundred dollars of what it would cost if I bought it on time."

Once you've led Sally into saying this, make it your basic point. Buying the car on time would cost you $9,834. Making your lease payments of $157.56 then buying it for $2,920 would total $10,482.88, or almost $650 more.

So ask what's going on. Did Sally Salespro tell you a fib? Are they trying to jerk you around, or what?

Politely accusing them of trying to cheat you will put considerable pressure on the manager to justify his figure.

To do that, he will have to tell you (a) that you're being charged a high rate of interest for a relatively small amount of money, or (b) that the buyout is set higher than it need be, preparing you to pay a profit you don't know about.

Obviously, he does not wish to utter those words, not even in his sleep. So he will have a problem. Keep this in mind to help bolster your self-confidence through all the bull.

End Game

And then begin the process of compromise that will help them save face. How? By repeating yourself, of course.

Say something like this: "Look, Sally said buying the car at the end would cost within a hundred of what it would cost to buy it in the first place. So the $2,920 is $650 too high. Take off the $650 and we have $2,270. I could see that, maybe even $2,300. Maybe another fifty for the paperwork."

Why offer more before they offer less? To get things rolling: to help the manager see a way to resolve the situation. You may be presenting these folks with something new. And when faced with something new, people sometimes freeze. Motion stops. Progress stops.

And progress should well be possible. For the manager's knowledge provides you with a lever. The manager knows, even though the salesperson may not, that the high buyout includes a future profit for the store.

However, he has a profit right now. And if you don't pay off the lease when it expires, the amount of the buyout is completely irrelevant. Why risk sure profit now to "secure" an extremely chancy profit in the future?

It doesn't make sense. Rather than risk losing certain money now, he should be willing to cut possible profit on a deal that may never happen—two or three or four years from now—when he may be working somewhere else anyway.

Make sure that this occurs to him. Point it out, if you have to. You may never buy the car anyway. The car will probably end up being returned to the lessor. Why risk blowing the deal now for a profit he may never see?

After you come to terms, the store will have to call the bank or credit company to see if they'll accept the contract with the lower buyout. A factory credit arm probably will. And so will a bank with which the store does considerable business. Some, however, will not. Then you simply compare the deal as it stands with the others you've found.

IF YOU WANT TO BUY A CAR YOU ARE CURRENTLY LEASING

Prepare as just described. Use lease payments and buy payments without taxes to do the calculations. If you can't find your old contract, break out the payment from the taxes by dividing the payment by 1.0X, where X equals the sales tax rate in your area. If, for example, your sales tax is 6% and your total payment is $200, divide 200 by 1.06 to get the lease payment of $188.68. As we just did, treat your payment—and the lender's return on investment—as an installment loan to establish a range of a couple hundred dollars within which you want the buyout to fall.

Then call your dealer or lease store. Get the name of the person you talk to. Get your buyout. Subtract $400 to $500. See how the resulting figure compares with the numbers in the range you have established.

Now call the lessor and try to obtain the buyout from them.

If they say they can't tell you, raise a little hell. Ask to whom you owe the money. Answer: You owe it to them, not to the dealer or the lease store. Therefore, you want the information from them, not the dealer or lease store.

When they say, "It's not our policy," or "Only the dealer has that information," ask for the supervisor. Tell the supervisor there's no way you're going to call the dealer. You want the information from the people you owe the money to. And if you don't get it, you are going to call your lawyer.

Normally, threatening people with your lawyer will not work unless you are rich. But give it a try. If it doesn't work, do it: Call a lawyer. There's probably nothing she can do and, given lawyer's fees, it probably wouldn't be cost-effective anyway, but the phone call is free and you have nothing to lose.

If this leads nowhere, it's time to visit the place you leased the car.

Your problem is that you signed a contract which includes a buyout. No one has to sell you the vehicle for anything less.

The Emotional Approach: Try to Bluff 'Em

Offer to buy out the lease for $400 less than the amount quoted. When they start arguing, tell them that you know they are tacking on a profit. Say that you're willing to pay a little profit, maybe a hundred or so, but you know they added a lot more than that. Tell them it's not legitimate, it's not fair, it's shady dealing, and you are very unhappy. Because nobody told you about this when you leased the car. Raise the question: Could that be fraud? Should you call your state attorney general and demand an investigation?

Feel free to get a little hot under the collar here. After all, you have a month or two left before you have to either pay up or relinquish the car.

The Rational Approach

If they stonewall you—or if you leased directly from a bank and there is no intermediary you can accuse of sleazing you into paying an unstated "fraudulent" profit—use the argument that if you don't buy the car, no one else may buy it, either.

After all, if you won't pay the buyout price, how do they know someone else will? They don't know. There's no way they can know. They may end up handing the car back to the lessor without making a nickel. (Or be stuck with it, if they're a bank.)

Yet here you are, right now, offering them a profit. And they don't have to do a thing—except give you an accurate buyout that includes a small profit, not a big one.

This is a logical and sensible argument. But since you've already signed a contract, you'd better be ready to negotiate. If you make no headway, suggest that you may be willing to settle for a little more. But not the buyout price; tell them it's way too high, a ridiculous price. You won't pay it and neither will anyone else.

Will this work?

When I explain how to negotiate a price and lease payment, I can assure you that it will work. If not the first time in the first store—not all stores deal, and some managers are nuts—then the second time in the second store.

But about negotiating a buyout, I can say only that sometimes it will and sometimes it won't.

Your chances of making it work, however, are good. You'll be dealing with retail stores in a highly competitive business. They need happy customers. They need good word-of-mouth advertising. And they know these things cost money.

On top of that, your argument is strong. A small profit today can be worth much more than a larger profit that they may never see.

And if you do make the negotiation work, you'll save hundreds of dollars.

Go for it.

EIGHT

A Few
Last Things

DEALING WITH IRRATIONAL MANAGERS

There is one thing that can screw up the works and be impossible to recognize while it's happening: Certain managers at certain times will not accept reasonable deals, let alone good ones. Behind the refusal lies anger, ego, or fear.

Sometimes a salesperson will do something that pisses off the manager. Then, amazing as it may seem, the manager may make the salesperson pay for her mistake by refusing a deal he'd normally take in a minute.

Sometimes the manager is just whacked out. One of our guys was a "big dude." On occasion, he'd decide the profit on a deal wasn't big enough for the size of his "dude-dom." And, bang, he'd turn it down. Wasting the salesman's time, the customer's time, and denying the house a deal.

And some managers simply don't have the self-confidence to take a deal when, as they say, it's all the way down to the bone. Put another way: when profit is so slim that the reason may have to be explained to the owner. Other managers, however, will take that kind of deal.

Try to go around a problem manager, not through him. If you are offering a small but reasonable profit and cannot get your deal accepted:

1. Ask the salesperson what the manager's problem is. She may know, and may tell you, for a salesperson's lot in life consists of trying to manipulate the manager at the same time she's trying to manipulate you.

2. Get another manager involved with the deal. If your salesperson doesn't think of this, tell her about it. Tell her to check with another manager, to get a second opinion on the value of your trade or the acceptability of the profit margin.

This may require either delicate diplomacy or considerable courage. If the salesperson feels she can't handle it, she may suggest that:

3. You leave and come back another day when another manager is available.

Sometimes these moves work. They've worked for me. But "come back another day" can also work as a ploy. You walk out. Then you come back, expecting a better deal. But all you can get is the same deal. The salesperson has had you put in more time; she's trying to wear you down.

Ask about this before agreeing to the tactic. And before you do come back, call the store. Make sure that the manager who is supposed to make you a better deal is there—and will still be there when you arrive.

DO YOUR HOMEWORK AND THEN TAKE YOUR TIME

It may sound as if you are in for a nightmare when you go out to lease a car. Not so. I've done lots of deals that were pleasant all the way through and resulted in good bargains and happy customers. In these instances, however, the customers almost always knew what they were doing and made sure they had plenty of time to do it.

This is important. Hurrying costs money. Once, after a friend had signed a contract on a Minivan, I went back to the store with her and saved her $324 in thirty minutes. Another thirty or forty minutes would have saved another $300. But my friend was on lunch hour and had to go back to work.

Before giving in to you and accepting your deal, the manager may need to think that both he and the salesperson have done a good job, have done everything they possibly can. This may take a while; both of them may have quite a number of moves to try. But time increases your bargaining power. The more time they spend on you, the more painful it is for them to lose the deal.

What are the chances you'll make a deal on your first visit? Good.

And even better than good if you are knowledgeable and firm. For the manager knows—and has told his salespeople over and over—that if you do walk, there's only one chance in ten that you will ever come back.

Even so, sometimes you have to walk out. A copy-machine sales manager leased a twelve-five Taurus from me at $269 over. To do it, he had to walk twice. And a friend of mine had to walk out twice before he got his price on a Mustang GT convertible. Nevertheless, both of them got the deals they wanted. And so will you.

Appendix A

The following are the residual value factors typical of those we used on deals financed through Ford Credit. They may have changed. Use them only for purposes of comparison and practice.

Residual Value Factors

Model	Lease Term			
	12	24	36	48
Escort	51	43	37	32
Escort EXP	50	42	36	30
Mustang LX	59	51	45	38
Mustang (other models)	55	48	41	35
Tempo	54	45	39	33
Taurus	57	50	44	36
Thunderbird	54	45	39	34
T-bird Turbo Coupe	50	41	34	30
Crown Victoria	55	45	37	31
Bronco	54	47	41	35

Residual Value Factors (*continued*)

Model	Lease Term			
	12	24	36	48
Bronco II	54	48	41	35
Aerostar	57	52	44	37
Econoline Van	54	47	40	33
Econoline Diesel	48	42	35	28
Ranger	57	48	42	35
Ranger Diesel	54	46	40	33
F-Series Pickup	54	47	40	33
Crew Cab	51	43	37	32
F-Series Diesel	47	41	34	28
Crew Cab	44	37	31	27

Factors are reduced 5 points for commercial use.

Appendix B

Here are some typical (at the time of this writing) residual value charts. They are from September to October 1988, the very beginning of the 1989 model year. With them, you can compare a couple of things: the residuals of the new '89s with the leftover '88s, and the difference between the residuals for '89 Fords and '89 Toyotas.

An atypical characteristic of these charts is that the Escorts have higher residuals than the Tauruses. If you were looking for an Escort, that would be good; if you were looking for a Taurus, you would be better off dealing through a lender who used higher residuals.

These charts have been compiled from those of different companies. No attempt has been made to bring them up-to-date. They are examples, to be used for practice only.

1989 MODELS

FORD	24 MO	36 MO	48 MO	60 MO
PROBE				
3d Hb GL	54%	46%	39%	34%
3d Hb LX	53%	46%	39%	33%
3d Hb GT	52%	44%	38%	33%
MUSTANG				
2d Sdn LX	53%	45%	38%	32%
2d Hb LX	53%	44%	37%	31%
2d Hb GT	55%	47%	39%	33%
2d Convertible GT	55%	47%	40%	33%
2d Convertible LX	52%	45%	38%	32%
deduct for manual transmission	4%	4%	3%	3%
TEMPO				
2d Cpe GL	47%	39%	32%	27%
4d Sdn GL	48%	40%	33%	27%
2d Cpe GLS	47%	39%	32%	26%
4d Sdn GLS	47%	39%	32%	26%
4d Sdn LX	46%	38%	31%	26%
4d Sdn 4WD	48%	40%	33%	27%
deduct for manual transmission	4%	4%	3%	3%
ESCORT				
2d Hb Pony	52%	44%	36%	30%
4d Hb LX	48%	41%	34%	28%
2d Hb LX	50%	42%	35%	29%
4d Wgn LX	48%	41%	34%	28%
2d Hb GT	50%	42%	35%	29%
deduct for Manual Trans (except GT)	4%	4%	3%	3%
TAURUS				
4d Sdn L	47%	40%	34%	28%
4d Wgn L 2s	46%	39%	33%	28%
4d Sdn GL	49%	42%	35%	30%
4d Wgn GL 2s	48%	41%	34%	29%
4d Sdn LX	45%	39%	32%	27%
4d Wgn LX 2s	46%	39%	33%	28%
4d Sdn SHO	46%	39%	33%	28%
deduct w/out air conditioning	4%	4%	3%	2%

1989 MODELS

FORD	24 MO	36 MO	48 MO	60 MO
LTD CROWN VICTORIA				
4d Sdn 'S'	51%	42%	34%	28%
4d Sdn	51%	42%	35%	28%
4d Wgn 2s	49%	41%	33%	28%
4d Wgn Country Sq 2s	49%	41%	33%	27%
4d Sdn LX	50%	42%	34%	28%
4d Wgn LX 2s	49%	41%	33%	27%
4d Wgn LX Country Sq 2s	49%	41%	33%	27%
THUNDERBIRD				
2d Coupe	50%	42%	36%	30%
2d Coupe LX	49%	42%	35%	30%
Super Coupe	48%	41%	35%	29%

FORD TRUCKS	24 MO	36 MO	48 MO	60 MO
E SERIES VAN				
E150 Van (All Models)	47%	40%	34%	29%
E150 Clb Wgn (All Models)	50%	42%	36%	30%
E250 Van (All Models)	47%	40%	34%	29%
E250 Clb Wgn (All Models)	50%	41%	35%	29%
E350 Van (All Models)	45%	39%	33%	27%
E350 Clb Wgn (All Models)	54%	47%	40%	33%
deduct for manual transmission	4%	4%	3%	3%
BRONCO II				
All Models	51%	44%	38%	32%
deduct for manual transmission	4%	4%	3%	3%
deduct for 2 Wheel Drive	6%	6%	5%	4%
BRONCO 4WD				
2d Wagon	49%	43%	36%	30%
deduct for manual transmission	4%	4%	3%	3%

Factors are reduced 10% for commercial use.

1989 MODELS (*continued*)

SUBARU	24 MO	36 MO	48 MO	60 MO
GL 10-XT6				
GL 10 4d Sdn	45%	36%	31%	26%
GL 10 4d Wgn	44%	37%	31%	26%
GL 10 4d Wgn 4WD Turbo	42%	36%	30%	25%
GL 10 4d Sdn 4WD Turbo	42%	35%	29%	24%
XT6 Cpe XT	45%	38%	31%	26%
XT6 Cpe XT 4WD	45%	38%	31%	26%
RX				
RX 3d Cpe 4WD Turbo	43%	36%	30%	25%
RX 4d Sdn 4WD Turbo	43%	36%	30%	25%

TOYOTA	24 MO	36 MO	48 MO	60 MO
TERCEL				
3d LB EZ	56%	48%	38%	33%
3d Lb	51%	43%	36%	30%
2d Cpe	55%	46%	39%	32%
2d Cpe Dlx	55%	47%	39%	32%
3d Lb Dlx	53%	45%	37%	31%
5d Lb Dlx	55%	46%	38%	32%
5d Wgn 4WD SR5	48%	41%	33%	28%
5d Wgn 4WD Dlx	48%	40%	34%	28%
COROLLA				
4d Sdn Dlx	56%	46%	39%	32%
5d Wgn Dlx	55%	46%	39%	32%
4d Sdn LE	53%	44%	37%	31%
2d Spt Cpe SR5	53%	44%	37%	31%
2d Spt Cpe GTS	49%	41%	34%	28%
4d Wgn Dlx 4WD	56%	47%	40%	34%
4d Wgn 4WD	56%	48%	40%	34%
COROLLA FX				
3d Lb FX	57%	48%	40%	33%
3d Lb FX-16	52%	44%	36%	30%
3d Lb FX-16 GTS	50%	42%	35%	29%
MR2				
2d Cpe	52%	45%	38%	33%
2d Supercharged Cpe	50%	43%	37%	31%

1989 MODELS (*continued*)

TOYOTA	24 MO	36 MO	48 MO	60 MO
CAMRY				
4d Sdn	62%	53%	46%	38%
4d Sdn Dlx	59%	52%	45%	40%
4d Sdn Dlx 4WD	58%	51%	44%	38%
4d Sdn LE	57%	50%	43%	37%
4d Sdn LE 4WD	55%	49%	42%	36%
5d Wgn Dlx	57%	50%	43%	37%
5d Wgn LE	55%	48%	42%	36%
CELICA				
2d Cpe ST	55%	47%	42%	36%
2d Cpe GTS	52%	45%	39%	34%
2d Cpe GT	52%	46%	39%	34%
3d Lb GTS	52%	45%	39%	33%
3d Lb GT	53%	46%	40%	34%
2d Convertible GT	52%	46%	40%	34%
3d Lb 4WD Turbo	56%	49%	42%	35%
CELICA SUPRA				
2d Lb Targa	52%	45%	40%	34%
2d Lb	52%	46%	39%	34%
2d Lb Turbo Targa	49%	43%	37%	32%
2d Lb Turbo	49%	43%	38%	33%

Factors reduced 8% for commercial use.

1988 MODELS

FORD	24 MO	36 MO	48 MO	60 MO
FESTIVA				
2d Hb L	40%	35%	29%	24%
2d Hb L Plus	40%	34%	28%	24%
2d Hb LX	40%	33%	28%	24%
ESCORT				
2d Hb Pony	44%	36%	30%	25%
2d Hb Pony (1988.5)	44%	36%	31%	26%
4d Hb GL	41%	34%	29%	24%
4d Hb LX (1988.5)	41%	34%	29%	24%
2d Hb GL	41%	34%	29%	24%

1988 MODELS (*continued*)

FORD	24 MO	36 MO	48 MO	60 MO
ESCORT				
2d Hb LX (1988.5)	43%	36%	30%	25%
4d Wgn GL	40%	33%	28%	24%
4d Wgn LX (1988.5)	41%	34%	28%	24%
2d Hb GT	42%	36%	30%	25%
2d Hb GT (1988.5)	43%	36%	30%	25%
deduct for manual trans (except GT)	4%	4%	3%	3%
EXP				
2d Luxury Cpe	41%	35%	28%	23%
2d Luxury Cpe (1988.5)	42%	36%	29%	24%
TEMPO				
2d Cpe GL	39%	33%	27%	22%
4d Sdn GL	40%	33%	27%	22%
2d Cpe GLS	39%	32%	26%	22%
4d Sdn GLS	39%	32%	26%	22%
4d Sdn LX	39%	33%	26%	21%
4d Sdn 4WD	40%	33%	27%	22%
deduct for manual transmission	5%	4%	3%	3%
TAURUS				
4d Sdn L	40%	34%	29%	24%
4d Wgn L 2s	39%	33%	28%	24%
4d Sdn MT5	37%	31%	27%	23%
4d Sdn GL	42%	36%	30%	25%
4d Wgn GL 2s	41%	35%	29%	25%
4d Sdn LX	39%	33%	28%	23%
4d Wgn LX 2s	39%	34%	28%	24%
deduct for manual trans (except MT5)	5%	4%	3%	3%
deduct w/out air conditioning	4%	4%	3%	3%
MUSTANG				
2d Sdn LX	45%	37%	32%	26%
2d Hb LX	44%	38%	32%	27%
2d Hb GT	47%	40%	34%	28%
2d Convertible GT	47%	41%	34%	30%
2d Convertible LX	45%	38%	32%	27%
deduct for manual transmission	4%	4%	3%	3%

1988 MODELS

FORD	24 MO	36 MO	48 MO	60 MO
LTD CROWN VICTORIA				
4d Sdn 'S'	41%	35%	28%	24%
4d Sdn	42%	35%	29%	24%
4d Wgn 2s	41%	34%	28%	23%
4d Wgn Country Sq 2s	41%	34%	28%	23%
4d Sdn LX	42%	35%	29%	24%
4d Wgn LX 2s	41%	34%	28%	23%
4d Wgn LX Country Sq 2s	41%	35%	28%	23%
THUNDERBIRD				
2d Coupe	40%	34%	29%	24%
2d Coupe Sport	39%	33%	30%	23%
2d Turbo Coupe	35%	30%	25%	21%
2d Coupe LX	41%	35%	29%	25%

FORD TRUCKS	24 MO	36 MO	48 MO	60 MO
BRONCO II				
All Models	44%	38%	34%	28%
deduct Manual Transmission	4%	4%	3%	3%
deduct 2 Wheel Drive	6%	6%	5%	4%

Factors are reduced 10% for commercial use.

Appendix C

Here are residual value factors combined from charts of lenders who at the time were very aggressively pursuing new business and using very high residuals to do it. The figures are from new model October charts, so the time of the year is the same as that of the 1989 model chart in Appendix B. Notice that the Taurus GL has a 48-month residual of 40% here as opposed to 35% there. This 5% difference would mean that a car with an MSRP of $15,000 leased through a lender using this chart would, all else being equal, have an acquisition cost $750 below the same car leased through a lender using Appendix B. The savings on the payment would be $18 a month or more. Get the *details* of the lease programs of different lenders.

Again, the figures have not been brought up to date. This is an example only.

FORD	24 MO	36 MO	48 MO	60 MO
BRONCO II				
2d Wgn 4WD	50%	44%	38%	31%
Eddie Bauer 4WD	45%	39%	33%	28%
BRONCO 4WD				
2d Cust Wgn 4WD	53%	44%	38%	32%
Eddie Bauer 4WD	48%	37%	34%	29%
AEROSTAR				
All Models	55%	47%	41%	36%
E SERIES VAN				
E150 van (All Models)	53%	44%	37%	31%
E250 Van (All Models)	52%	43%	38%	30%
E350 Van (All Models)	51%	43%	38%	30%
F SERIES PICKUP				
F150 Reg Cab (All Models)	54%	45%	37%	31%
F150 Suprcab (All Models)	49%	41%	34%	29%
F250 Reg Cab (All Models)	52%	44%	37%	31%
F250 Suprcab (All Models)	48%	40%	33%	28%
F350 Reg Cab (All Models)	52%	42%	35%	30%
F350 Crw Cab (All Models)	47%	39%	34%	27%
RANGER PICKUP				
Reg Cab (All Models)	58%	48%	41%	35%
Suprcab (All Models)	53%	47%	39%	33%

Reduce truck factors 10% for commercial use.

	24 MO	36 MO	48 MO	60 MO
ESCORT				
2d Hb Pony	51%	44%	39%	32%
4d Hb GL	51%	44%	39%	32%
2d Hb GL	51%	44%	39%	33%
4d Wgn GL	51%	44%	39%	33%
2d Hb GT	51%	44%	39%	33%
EXP				
2d Hb Lux Cpe	49%	43%	35%	30%
2d Hb Spt Cpe	49%	42%	34%	30%
TEMPO				
2d Cpe GL	52%	44%	39%	35%
4d Sdn GL	53%	45%	40%	35%

FORD	24 MO	36 MO	48 MO	60 MO
2d Cpe LX	50%	43%	37%	32%
4d Sdn LX	50%	43%	37%	32%
TAURUS				
4d Sdn L	54%	46%	39%	34%
4d Wgn L	55%	47%	40%	35%
4d Sdn MT5	55%	47%	40%	35%
4d Wgn MT5	53%	46%	39%	34%
4d Sdn GL	55%	47%	40%	35%
4d Wgn GL	55%	47%	40%	35%
4d Sdn LX	55%	47%	40%	35%
4d Wgn LX	55%	47%	40%	35%
MUSTANG				
2d Cpe LX	58%	52%	45%	39%
3d Hb LX	58%	52%	45%	39%
3d Hb GT	55%	50%	40%	35%
2d Conv GT	55%	50%	40%	35%
2d Conv LX	55%	50%	40%	35%
THUNDERBIRD				
2d Cpe	53%	45%	40%	33%
2d Tbo Cpe	45%	39%	34%	29%
2d Cpe LX	53%	45%	40%	33%
CROWN VICTORIA				
4d 'S' Sdn	48%	39%	32%	28%
2d Cpe	50%	40%	34%	29%
4d Sdn	50%	40%	34%	29%
4d 'S' Wgn	45%	35%	30%	28%
4d Wgn	50%	40%	34%	30%
4d Wgn Cntry Sq 2s	50%	40%	34%	30%
2d Cpe LX	50%	40%	34%	29%
4d Sdn LX	50%	40%	34%	29%
4d Wgn LX	50%	40%	34%	29%
4d Wgn LX Cntry Sq	50%	41%	34%	30%

Reduce all vehicle factors 14% for diesel engines.

Glossary

Actual cash value (*cash value*)—The amount a used car can be sold for immediately; the wholesale value. Based on the automobile auction prices of the specific make and model with its specific options.

Acquisition cost—Leasing's equivalent to the principal on a loan. Based on the purchase price, with various additions for fees, insurance, maintenance contracts, and any other extras you purchase, and subtractions for cash down and trade allowance, this is the amount that the lender/lessor advances the dealer to acquire the car; the price that you have negotiated to acquire the lease, a part of which you are obliged to pay back. See CAPITALIZED COST.

Amortize—To pay off in periodic installments. The period is usually monthly, the installments usually of the same size.

APR (*Annualized Percentage Rate*)—The total cost of your loan, including fees, points, and any other charges, expressed as a percentage rate, or an annual interest rate. If a lender charges you a $50 up-front application fee to lend you $1,000 for one year, then charges only 8% interest (in an 11% market—which was what attracted you to that lender), you would pay back $86.99 a month, as if you had been lent

$1,000. But you haven't; you've been lent $950. You traded $50 for $1,000, ending up with $950 more than you started with.

The total cost to you for the use of that $950 would be $93.88. ($86.99 × 12 = $1,043.88 − $950 = $93.88.)

Now, if you didn't have to pay back the $950 till the end of the twelfth month, your interest rate would be $93.88 ÷ 950 = .09882, or a little over 9 $7/8$%. But since you are paying back more than $80 of the $950 principal every month, the APR calculated on the declining balance would be over 17.75%.

Scams like this were once common, bringing about the truth-in-lending laws that require disclosure of APR.

Balance subject to lease charges—(a) The depreciation plus the residual value, or the total amount on which interest is charged. Another way to look at this is the total amount of money the bank considers itself to own. (b) Some lenders, however, like General Electric Credit, use this phrase as a synonym for acquisition cost and/or capitalized cost.

Book value—What an industry standard used-car price guide says a car is worth at wholesale. Some give retail values, but retail prices are hard to average in any meaningful way.

Book—Short for "book value."

Big book—Worth an unusually large amount, as in "the Boomer Turbo Twelve has a big book."

Bump—Noun: a price increase. Verb: to increase the price; to persuade a customer to pay more.

Capitalized cost (also **Cap cost**)—In most lease contracts, the same as acquisition cost: purchase price plus any extras or lender fees minus anything put down.

Capitalized cost reduction—Cash or trade equity put down on the leased car, lowering the capitalized cost or acquisition cost.

Cash difference—The selling price of a new car minus the trade allowance for the customer's old car.

Cost—What an object costs the person who sells it to you.

Invoice cost—The amount the factory invoice says the dealer has to pay for the car. In this book, we use "invoice cost" to include finance charges the dealer must pay, whether or not they appear on the invoice. Sometimes known as "dead cost."

Dealer cost—What the dealer has on his books as cost after the addition of an amount for overhead, usually called the pack or pac, sometimes called a "lot charge," or "lot fee" (as in parking lot).

Depreciation—Loss in value owing to time, use, and wear and tear. Also, in auto leasing, the estimated amount of that loss over the time your lease will run; and the part of your monthly lease payment that pays off the amount.

F & I Guy, a.k.a. Business Manager or Finance Manager—F stands for "finance," I for "insurance." The person at a dealership who places customer lease or purchase financing, prepares contracts, arranges liability and collision insurance if purchased through the dealership, and, increasingly, sells the after-sale items, such as rustproofing, paint and fabric guard, credit life and disability insurance—and has a computer on his desk to confuse you about the price you're paying for these things.

Floorplan—Dealership financing for the purchase of new cars from the manufacturer.

Gross, grosses, the gross—Profit on the sale of a car after its cost and the pack have been subtracted but before subtraction of sales commissions and most other expenses.

Hard dollars—The amount of money, normally a portion of the trade allowance, that a dealership invests in a trade-in, the amount actually paid for a trade-in. Contrasts with "show dollars," the portion of a trade allowance consisting of a discount off the sticker price of a new car.

Interest—Money charged for the use of someone else's money, which, strictly speaking, you do not pay on a lease because you are using someone else's car, not their money. This is a form of hairsplitting brought about by the legal distinctions between leasing and installment sales.

LAH—Credit life, accident, and health insurance. Insures the lender against your failing to pay owing to injury, sickness, or death. Some dealerships will be kind enough to include LAH in your payment (lease or buy) without your asking for it.

Lease charges—Leasing's name for interest.

Lemon law—A law, usually at the state level, requiring used cars sold to the public to be halfway drivable. If they aren't, the dealer is required to fix the car or take it back. (How drivable a car must be varies from place to place, as does the existence of the law.)

    Lemon law warranty—A warranty required by the lemon law on used cars. It stipulates what is covered, the amount of the deductible, and how long coverage lasts.

Lender—Generic name for institutions that lend money.

Lessee—The person (or company) that leases a car. You.

Lessor—The company that buys the car, then leases it to you. In most consumer leasing of vehicles for personal use, the lender is or becomes (after assignment of the lease) the lessor.

Lien—A legal, court-enforceable claim to ownership arising through a debt. Liens must be recorded in writing, either on the title or on some other state or county document.

List price—Sticker price. In our terms here, MSRP (see separate entry) after factory discounts.

    "Lists for"—Carries a sticker price of.

    MSRP (Manufacturer's Suggested Retail Price)—What the manufacturer suggests the car be sold for. In this book, we are restricting the meaning to the manufacturer's suggested price before the manufacturer's discount(s) for options packages. If a car has no packages or no discounts, that restriction becomes unnecessary, for then MSRP and sticker price are identical.

Options package—A number of equipment options sold as a group; a.k.a. "options group." The point of grouping the options is to sell the package for a kind of bulk-buying discounted price that is less than the total of the retail prices of all the options in the group.

    Options package discount—The discount.

    Package discount—Ditto.

Pack or *Pac*—An amount an auto dealer adds to invoice cost to cover overhead. Sometimes referred to as "lot charge."

Purchase option—A clause in a lease contract that gives you the right to buy the car. The time at which you may exercise the option and the price you must pay to do it are usually, but not necessarily, specified in the contract.

Rat, roach, pig, sled—Your trade-in. "Derog.," as they say in dictionaries.

Residual Value—The dollar value amount that the lender/lessor expects the car to be worth at the end of the lease.

Residual Value Factor—A percentage, usually of the MSRP before factory discounts, which is used to determine a car's residual value.

Retail—Sticker price, list price. The MSRP after options package or other factory discounts.

A retail price—Any price for which a retail outlet sells a car to the public.

"Retails for"—Carries a sticker price of.

Show dollars—Dealer discount off the sticker price of a new car which is shown as money paid for a trade-in. See HARD DOLLARS.

Sticker price—The MSRP after manufacturer's discounts are subtracted from the original MSRP. These discounts will be shown on the window sticker; the manufacturer wants you to be aware of the bargain you are getting.

Trade allowance—The total amount shown as paid for a trade-in and subtracted from the price of a new car.

Trade equity—The amount of a trade-in's value over and above the amount owed on it.

Use tax—In some states, leasing's equivalent of sales tax; sales tax with a different name, made necessary because a lease is not, strictly speaking, a sale to you, and lessors have the wholesale distributors' exemption from sales taxes.

Wholesale, wholesale value—The amount a used car has been bringing at auction sales, usually no longer ago than the previous week. See ACTUAL CASH VALUE.

Index

9936

13.80